Growing
Roses

Publisher and Creative Director: Nick Wells
Senior Project Editor: Catherine Taylor
Art Director: Mike Spender
Layout Design: Jane Ashley
Digital Design & Production: Chris Herbert
Copy Editor: Anna Groves
Proofreader: Dawn Laker
Indexer: Helen Snaith

Special thanks to: Ilana Davis, Eleanor Chitty, Helena Keeble, Frances Bodiam.

FLAME TREE PUBLISHING
6 Melbray Mews, Fulham
London SW6 3NS
United Kingdom

First published 2019
© 2019 Flame Tree Publishing Ltd

23 22 21 20 19
10 9 8 7 6 5 4 3 2 1

ISBN 978-1-78755-271-5

A CIP record for this book is available from the British Library upon request.

Picture credits: Courtesy of Shutterstock.com and © the following: Sergey Pikalo 1; Preecha Ngamsrisan 3 & 67br; Baranov E 4tl & 19; Julietphotography 5cr & 115; Olga_Ionina 5tl & 81, 70tl, 143, 169; Peter Turner Photography 5b & 135 & 138, 14tl, 39cr, 90, 117, 118br, 129cr, 145tr, 145br; OlgaNik 6tl & 159; Robert Przybysz 6br & 181; Rimma Bondarenko 7bl & 240; S.O.E 7tr & 203 & 214; ArtCookStudio 10bl; oksana2010 10tr; Aksiniya Art 11, 103; Del Boy 12bl, 41tr, 58tl, 89, 99, 100bl, 132, 148, 178; Svetlana8Art 12tr; Hannamariah 13, 130; VICUSCHKA 14br; Piccia Neri 15; Slavica Stajic 16cr; vseb 16tr; marilyn barbone 20; OKcamera 21tr; Shebeko 21cr; Vastram 21bl; Africa Studio 22bl, 228bl, 236; ueuaphoto 22tr; mountainpix 23; 123dartist 24tl; mgallar 24br; Rana Des 25; Nagel Photography 26; Lindsay Jubeck 27; Katya123ua 28bl; Lijphoto 28tl; AnastasiaKopa 29br; marypastukh 29tr; Graeme Dawes 30tl, 197; Paul Atkinson 30cr, 68cl, 100tl, 250; bkel 33; Johnnie Martin 34br, 46br, 50tl, 65tr, 65cr, 67cl, 69tr, 75bl, 75cr, 76cr; Serhii Dubenets 34tl; Katarzyna Klimasz 35; PhotoHouse 36; aclaire 37l; BeppeNob 37cr; feathercollector 37tr; Manfred Ruckszio 38cl, 77tr, 164, 210, 212; Vahan Abrahamyan 38bl; EQRoy 39br; victimewalker 39bl; Ilona5555 40tl; neil hardwick 40cl; Svetoslav Radkov 40bl; JurateBuiviene 41bl, 46tr, 48tr; Xzelen Rain 41cr; Benedictus

42bl; ChWeiss 42br, 38tl; Matt Hudson 42tl; Nikolay Kurzenko 42cl; David Byron Keener 43cr; Mary Lane 43cl; Myrox 43br;creativeness 44tr; Noppharat4969 44bl; karinabilder 45cr, 45br; RukiMedia 45tr, 56cl; Andrea Mangoni 46tl; Ole Schoener 46bl, 47br, 74, 109tr, 147cr; marinatakano 47tl, 47bl, 60cl, 100cl, 104br, 200, 208tr; unoeh 47tr, 51cr; avoferten 48bl; Coastal Girl 48cl; LagunaticPhoto 50tr; LianeM 50cl, 249; JohannesOehl 51bl; ajisai13 52cr; Colette3 52cr; lavenderblue 52tr; Margo Harrison 53cr; Ohhlanla 53br; Tasa-fw 53bl; ata_moro 54bl; RealityImages 54cr, 191; Tom Curtis 57br, 67tl; adrianadefernex 58bl; Sourav Tarafder 58cl; milmed 59tr; SJ Allen 59cr; Nele Curwood 60bl; photowind 61tr, 61br, 206; Bonnie Taylor Barry 62cl; Katarzyna Mazurowska 62br; iceink 63cr; Drew Rawcliffe 64cl; Monika Pa 65tl, 75tl, 76br, 105; Besklubova Liubov 66tl, 75br; Jane McIlroy 66bl; Ann in the uk 68tl; Wicked Digital 69cr; InfoFlowersPlants 72bl, 144bl; Bildagentur Zoonar GmbH 73br, 76cl, 223; David OBrien 75tr, 108; Lflorot 77tl; V J Matthew 77cr, 162; Alenka Krek 78br; Gerry Burrows 78tr; Lesley Rigg 78cr; Marina Rose 78bl; iMarzi 82; ALPA PROD 83;triff 84; Roger de Montfort 86; Khrystyna Bohush 87; Alina G 88; PhotoJuli86 91; joloei 92bl, 182; Julia Kuleshova 92cr, 125br; Ania K 93tr; Ketrin_Ti 93bl, 151; Kritchai7752 94; patjo 96; Pereslavtseva Katerina 97; Alison Rifici 98r; Dorothy Chiron 98l; smoxx 100br; YukoF 100tr, 106; Rogatnykh 101; Chris Hiill 102; Nix Sallihen 104tr; 1000 Words 107; Elena Glezerova 109br, 209; Pedrag Lukic 110; Maljalen 111; Ratchanee Sawasdijira 116; Raffaella Galvani 118tl; Shahar Shabtai 119; Heller Joachim 120; ESB Basic 121; Harry Wedzinga 123; Anna Tkach 124bl; Christian Mueller 124tr; Steve Heap 125tr; Soohyun Kim 126; Milleflore Images 127; Douglas Barclay 128tl; Joshua Haviv 128bl; Bbrown 129tr; Yolanta 129br; Shelli Jensen 131; Moskwa 136; wjarek 137;blacky111 139tr; Jacqui Martin 139br; Natalia Greeske 140; Hama-Kid 141tr; Jayne Newsome 141bl; kuni---ka 144tr; alybaba 146cr; Zummolo 148cr; greeninthebox 147tr; loretagema 149, 155; StockOption 150tr; U.klinger 150bl; krolya25 152tr; Studio Grand Quest 152bl; Rtimages 154tr;bleakstar 160; Andrii Zastrozhnov 161br; Cheng Yi 161tr; angelaflu 163; Bob Mawby 165cr; Milos Luzanin 165bl; Jinga 166; alicja neumiler 167tr; stockcreations 167bl, 193; bane.m 170cl; SujaImages 170tl; Evtushkova Olga 172bl; Jorge Salcedo 173; roibu 174; TCGraphicDesign 176tl; StellaBeePhotography 177; Luca9257 183; Jim Elve 184; Marynka Mandarinka 185; Kostenko Maxim 186bl; tesoro-photo 187; dkingsleyfish 188; SIM ONE 189; LDprod 190; Radovan1 194, 198, 205br; Jaruek Chairak 195cl; JustinVa 195tr; perfectlab 196; susanna mattioda 199; Khairil Azhar Junos 204; STEVENSON 205tl; MaryAnne Campbell 208bl; mykhailo pavlenko 211tl; rck_953 213; AlexBuess 215tl; Henri Koskinen 215br; Tomasz Klejdysz 216cl, 216bl; windsketch 216tl; Pete Pahham 217br; topseller 217tr; ninii 218; Maren Winter 219br; Tonkovic 220; Ellica 224;crayOnLine 225bl; JSOBHATIS16899 225tr; Ellie.tuang 226tr; mari-s 226bl; Daria_Cherry 227; Sergeyclocikov 228tr; Mirage_studio 229; 3DE Studios 230br; Rawpixel.com 230tl; vanillaechoes 231; Jarek Sobel 232tr; Prostock-studio 232br; vesna cvorovic 233bl; Victoria Tucholka 233tr; natalia bulatova 234br; Sebastiana 234cr; Kvitka Fabian 235; StockphotoVideo 237; Lyuba Alex 238; Skripnik Olga 242; glebchik 243; Dervin Witmer 244; OlgaPonomarenko 245; VitCOM Photo 246; Bobkov Evgeniy 247; Tatiana Kholina 248. **Courtesy of The Real Flower Company** (©): 8, 9. **Wikimedia Commons and the following:** A. Barra/GNU Free Documentation License 37br, 58tr; Yuriy75/Attribution-ShareAlike 3.0 Unported (CC BY-SA 3.0) 39tr; T.Kiya/Attribution-ShareAlike 2.0 Generic (CC BY-SA 2.0) 53bl, 71; Stickpen/CC0 1.0 Universal (CC0 1.0), Public Domain Dedication 55tr. **Courtesy of GAP Photos and the following:** Charles Hawes 38tr, 53cl; Benedikt Dittli 45b; Howard Rice 48tl, 49cr, 50bl, 54br, 55tl, 56br, 60br, 63tl, 153;clive Nichols 49tr, 52tl; Maddie Thornhill 49tl, 55bl, 56tl; Juliette Wade 50br; Suzie Gibbons 51tr; Maxine Adcock 56tl; Richardbloom 56bl, 156tr; Rob Whitworth 57tr, 65bl, 72br; Pernilla Bergdahl 58br, 142; Jo Whitworth 59bl; Christina Bollen 61bl; Neil Holmes 61cr; Heather Edwards 63tr; John Glover 63bl, 122; Dave Zubraski 64br, 66br, 68bl, 68br; – 67bl, 72cl, 176bl, 186tr; Nicola Stocken 70br, 147cl; Ron Evans 70bl, 95; Visions 70tr; FhF Greenmedia 72tr, 73tr, 73cr; Jonathan Buckley 78tr; Elke Borkowski 154bl; Graham Strong 156bl; Friedrich Strauss 168tl, 173, 207, 239; Michael King 172tr; Marcus Harpur 219tl. **Flickr/CC0 1.0 Universal (CC0 1.0), Public Domain Dedication:** Bernard Spragg. NZ 70cl; Scot Nelson 216br. **Courtesy of David Austin Roses** (©): 168tl, 168bl, 170bl, 171tr, 171cr. **Courtesy of Rex/Shutterstock/FLPA/Nigel Cattlin:** 211br.

Growing Roses

JENNY HENDY

Foreword by Rosebie Morton, founder of The Real Flower Company

FLAME TREE
PUBLISHING

Contents

The combination of roses' beautiful form, colour and fragrance has always been a draw. In this chapter, we dip into roses of the ancient world, where wild species provided not only foodstuffs, medicines and perfumes but were also symbolic and woven into myths and legends. For some, roses became an obsession, no more so than Empress Josephine's pivotal early-nineteenth-century collection at Malmaison. The enduring appeal of roses, including rose naming and the rose as a token of love and romance, is also explored.

Roses spread across the northern hemisphere as they evolved, mostly colonizing temperate regions. We start by looking at some of the 350 wild rose species found in North America, Asia, Europe and North Africa. Species valued by early civilizations are listed, as well as any important in rose breeding. Old Garden Rose descriptions and snippets from their fascinating history take the reader to the Modern roses. Some of the best examples of these, including disease-resistant bush, shrub, climbing and ground-cover types, provide a colourful taster.

Where to Grow Roses . . . .

In this chapter, the effects of climate, aspect, soil type and drainage are explored with respect to rose growing, along with all the other factors affecting your choice of where and what to grow. The reader is encouraged to discover potential sites around the garden, weighing advantages and disadvantages. Rose lists are provided for more challenging soils and conditions. We look at roses suitable for containers, for covering walls and structures and for planting in borders or for flowering hedges. There's advice on roses for period or formal gardens through to ones suitable for wild or country plantings.

Designing with Roses. . .

Here, the footprint or underlying bones of a garden are discussed and ways to achieve the desired look or feel, including colour scheming, adding structures and creating focal points. The various styles of gardens used for rose growing, along with their signature elements and construction materials, are presented in easy-to-follow points, whether you prefer formal or relaxed, vintage or contemporary. There are ideas for incorporating fragrant roses around the house and for making the most of small spaces.

Rose Companions . . . .

Roses look even better when they have a supporting cast. Taking into account the form of rose bushes and the shape and texture of the blooms, you can select flowers and foliage to offer a pleasing contrast. Classic companions include daisy-like blooms; tall, slender foxgloves, delphiniums and salvias; frothy catmint and lady's mantle; and bell-, bowl- or funnel-shaped blooms such as campanula, geranium and penstemon. We also include climbing-rose companions and foliage and bulbs to extend the season.

Buying & Planting Roses 158

For roses to perform to their best ability, good ground preparation and correct planting depth are vital. Bare-root grafted or budded roses as well as 'own root' roses and hedging, often purchased by mail order, are lifted and planted in winter. These usually establish more quickly than the more expensive container-grown roses purchased from garden centres and nurseries, and can go in the ground any time, soil and weather conditions allowing. This chapter also looks at planting climbers and potted Patio roses.

Caring for Your Roses 180

Ways to reduce the stress on new plantings and how to speed up establishment are explored here. Pointers include watering requirements for new roses as well as routine watering for containers and for areas with dry summers. Mulching helps to manage moisture conservation, provide nutrients, control weeds and certain pests and diseases. Additional rose-specific feeding information is also given. Pruning different types of roses, starting with the basics of maintaining rose health, expands into pruning and training to maximize flowering.

Pests & Problems 202

Roses can be grown within a wide range of temperature and humidity variables if you choose the right varieties. Here, we suggest roses for more extreme circumstances as well as preparing roses in borders and containers for approaching cold winters. Many problems are reduced by following good cultivation practices, producing strong-growing roses. The book follows an environmentally friendly approach throughout and here, guidelines are given for controlling common pests and diseases such as aphids and black spot.

Taking Things Further 222

Growing your own roses for cutting is a treat and here, techniques for small-scale growing and preparing roses are included as well as ideas for simple arrangements. You can also dry whole roses and rose petals for a variety of decorative uses and make your own rose-petal confetti or potpourri. Organically grown roses are edible and here, recipes for rose-flavoured sugar, ice cream and rose water are given as well as ways to garnish and decorate cakes and desserts and create eye-catching centre-pieces.

Foreword

No other flower in history has been so loved, discussed and fought over as the rose. Even now, it is still recognized as the most popular flower in the world. Fossils of roses date back 35 million years, but roses only became fashionable in the West in the 1800s, when roses imported from China were crossed with European cultivars, leading to the colourful, repeat-flowering forms we have today.

Gardening in the twenty-first century has changed immeasurably from when these first roses were introduced. In the Victorian period, they were often grown in formal and stiff-looking rose beds, which required diligent handling, including copious spraying, pruning and general maintenance. Today's

8

gardeners do not have the time or the inclination to grow roses in this manner. Other floral factors such as health, vigour and a long flowering season have become much more important; at the same time, so has care for the environment and valuing biodiversity. Growing roses in mixed planting schemes is more wildlife-friendly and will encourage many more birds and beneficial insects. Space is also often limited, so roses need to be able to flourish along with other flowers and shrubs.

Choosing the right roses can be incredibly daunting and the wrong choice can lead to a sad and sickly rose. This book gives you a comprehensive guide to picking the right varieties of roses for every aspect, together with ideas for companion plants which grow well amongst roses, whilst the text still leaves room for, and indeed inspires, the reader's imagination. Gardens and outside spaces of all shapes and sizes are catered for, proving that gardens come in many different guises and that roses, whether grown in a window box or a border, are for everyone.

We are hugely demanding of our roses, requiring them to flower continuously, smell exquisite and require minimal effort. However, with the right care, they can. Jenny Hendy's book provides the reader with all the information to achieve just this.

Rosebie Morton
The Real Flower Company

Introduction

The history of rose growing and use by man for spiritual, medicinal and culinary reasons, as a source of fragrance and for decorations and celebrations goes back thousands of years. This is certainly part of their enduring appeal, but the rose is having a renaissance amongst today's gardeners attracted by the colour range, beauty and fragrance of the blooms as well as their incredibly long flowering period.

Straightforward Approach

Modern trends in rose growing are following those of gardening in general – enjoy more and work less! You do not need special knowledge or skills and rose growing is now less rigid and more adaptable.

These days, it is possible to minimize or avoid the use of pesticides on roses

▶ **Labour saving:** There are simple cultivation methods that cut down on feeding, watering and weeding and some single-bloomed roses do not need deadheading.

▶ **Green credentials:** Roses once had a strict spraying regime, but growing roses amongst other plants, using organic methods and encouraging natural predators keeps time spent on pest and disease control to a minimum. Many modern roses have built-in resistance.

▶ **Basic rose know-how:** Follow the step-by-step directions for planting, feeding, pruning and training in this book and roses will reward you. Rose cultivation terms are explained and jargon kept to a minimum. You just need to pick suitable roses for your conditions and size of garden or container. This book provides information and inspiration for both. There are also 'checklists' at the end of each chapter, which highlight the main points.

The Versatile Rose

Roses are tough survivors that reward any extra effort that you put into them. Their fragrance alone makes them worthy of cultivation. This book demonstrates the diversity and versatility of roses. It shows how well Modern roses, as well as several historic cultivars, fit into today's hectic lifestyle and smaller garden plots. There are species and varieties to suit any garden situation and, if the thorns have ever put you off growing these generous-blooming beauties, there are even smooth-stemmed cultivars.

Rosa 'Crown Princess Margareta' is a near-thornless rose

Worldwide Appeal

Although roses originated in the northern hemisphere, they are now grown worldwide in a range of climate zones from areas with freezing winters to sub-tropical and desert locations. This book encourages readers to seek out their best local roses, as well as pointing out groups of roses that work well in more challenging regions or soil types. The second chapter, 'A Gallery of Roses', lays out the main groups, detailing their history and attributes, and includes recent trends in breeding.

Seasons

In this book, we have avoided specifying months, because the months of the seasons are reversed between the northern and the southern hemispheres, so:

Many roses can survive tough conditions

▶ **Early, mid- and late spring** = March, April and May *in the northern hemisphere*, or September, October and November *in the southern hemisphere*.

▶ **Early, mid- and late summer** = June, July and August; *or* December, January and February.

▶ **Early, mid- and late autumn** = September, October and November; *or* March, April and May.

▶ **Early, mid- and late winter** = December, January and February; *or* June, July and August.

Roses for Everyone

Old garden roses, often called heritage or antique roses, have a reputation for being prima donnas, but in fact several groups in this category are drought- or shade-resistant and tolerant of poor or dry soils. Many modern repeat-flowering (remontant), disease-resistant roses

A riot of red in a mixed border of canna, roses, fuchias and dahlias

have been bred with vintage looks, perfect for the romantic soul who also wants an easy life. In the third chapter, 'Where to Grow Roses', a variety of locations are explored, with numerous examples to get you started.

Here is a brief summary of the wide range of gardens and gardening styles that would be enhanced by the addition of roses:

▶ **Mixed borders:** Most people fill their beds and borders with an assortment of plants, and in smaller gardens, every one has to earn its place. There are compact, long-flowering and disease-resistant roses to suit any colour scheme.

▶ **Shrub borders:** These are becoming popular again because of their easy maintenance, and Modern Shrub roses fit right in.

▶ **Formal gardens:** Ideal for houses with a period feel, you can include well-behaved Old Garden roses or vintage lookalikes as well as elegant standard roses. Climbers, including spectacular Ramblers, soften formal structures.

▶ **Cottage gardens:** The country charm and wildlife-friendly character of many Modern Shrub roses and single- or semi-double-flowered Floribundas make them ideal candidates here. **Note:** 'Double' flowers have many more petals than the 'single' form of the flower, while 'semi-double' vary in petal number but still have an open centre showing the stamens.

▶ **Wild or country gardens:** Well-behaved wild roses as well as single- or semi-double-flowered shrub roses that repeat bloom all season are perfect for the semi-wild or larger country garden. Insect pollinators, birds and mammals are attracted by the abundant flowers and hips.

▶ **Hedges:** Low to medium-sized flowering hedges are a huge bonus in gardens lacking summer and autumn colour and make pretty garden dividers. Many, like the Rugosa hybrids, produce fruits and have handsome, disease-resistant foliage too.

▶ **Containers:** Provided the pot is big enough, you can successfully grow all but the most vigorous roses, including climbers. This opens up paved areas and decks to roses, bringing fragrance close to the house.

▶ **Courtyards:** Miniature climbers, Patio and Miniature roses fit neatly in confined spaces such as raised beds. No garden is too small for roses. You can even grow them on a balcony.

▶ **Easy-care landscapes:** Single-flowered shrub roses that do not need deadheading, as well as groundcover or landscaping roses that spread effortlessly over large areas of ground, are easy to maintain. Many are a little shade- and drought-tolerant too once established, and can even be cut with shears or an electric hedge-trimmer.

▶ **Vertical gardening:** Climbers and Ramblers utilize vertical garden space such as walls and fences and artfully cover arbours, archways, pergolas and obelisks.

Mix 'n' Match

Not so long ago, growing roses in isolation was the norm, for bush roses in particular. But these colourful flowering shrubs work so much better with complementary or contrasting plant partners. There is even evidence to suggest that they are healthier grown like this. This book shows you how to design with roses and how to combine them with a wide range of plants, including herbaceous perennials, shrubs and summer bulbs. See chapter five, 'Rose Companions'.

Taking Things Further

Roses are a much-loved florist's flower, with strong links to romantic occasions such as weddings. Our final chapter shows how to get the best from your home-grown blooms, with tips on making them last longer as well as step-by-step instructions for simple arrangements. There are numerous less well-known uses for roses too and the following decorative and culinary applications are explored:

▶ **Drying roses:** We show you how to make rose confetti, potpourri and whole dried blooms.

▶ **Rose water:** We have included an ancient technique that yields rose-scented liquid for flavouring foods.

▶ **Decorating cakes:** You can make crystallized or candied rose petals and buds, which you can use along with fresh petals for decorations and garnishes.

▶ **Rose sugar:** We show you a simple technique for capturing the scent of roses in sugar for cooking and flavouring.

▶ **Ice bowl:** Flowers suspended in ice make an eye-catching dinner party centrepiece.

▶ **Rose dessert:** Prepare your own delicately flavoured rose petal ice cream to capture the essence of summer.

Understanding Nomenclature

A final word on plant names. You will notice that the names of roses (indeed, all plants) are written in a certain way. We have followed convention, whilst trying to keep things simple for the reader:

▶ **Genus:** This is a collective name for a group of plants, and is written in 'Botanical Latin' and in italics – in this case, all roses fall under the genus *Rosa* (which, you will see, we often abbreviate to *R.* to avoid repetition). (Incidentally, ranking *above* the genus is the family. Here, *Rosa* is part of the family *Rosaceae.*)

▶ **Specific name:** This is another name that follows the genus, and together with the genus tells you what the species is. So, for example, the word '*gallica*' in *Rosa gallica*.

▶ **Subspecies and variety:** Further subdivisons known as 'subspecies' and 'varieties' may follow the specific name, also in Latin and often prefixed by the non-italic abbreviations 'subsp.' and 'var.' respectively. So, for example, *Rosa stellata* var. *mirifica*. A true 'variety' is one that is found in the wild, relating directly to a species. However, people will often speak of 'varieties' when really, they mean 'cultivars'.

▶ **Cultivar:** This word comes from the combination of the words 'cultivated' and 'variety' – in other words, developed by man. The cultivar name is *not* in Latin or italics, and is usually in single quotation marks. So, for example, *Rosa* 'Rêve d'Or'. However, in our entries in bold, we have dispensed with the quotation marks for the sake of tidiness.

▶ **Commercial names:** Plants sold internationally are often given different names to the original cultivar by the various retailers. These are not usually written in single quotes. However, for simplicity, we have followed the convention for cultivars and have only dropped the quotes for commercial series such as the Knock Out® roses.

▶ **Hybrids:** When different species or varieties are cross-bred to create new plants, they are hybrids. A hybrid is indicated by the use of the multiplication sign ('×'), for example, *R.* × *alba* is a hybrid of *R. gallica* and *R. canina*.

▶ **Common and other names:** Then there are of course other names, used without italics or even capitals. For example, rose species names can be used as group names – such as 'Centifolia roses', also known as 'Provence roses'; or *R. gallica* 'Officinalis' is also called the apothecary's rose or the crimson Damask rose.

The Allure
of Roses

A Deep Connection

Roses are woven through our history. Man has used roses for medicines and perfumes, for food and flavourings. People have taken roses with them wherever they have travelled and set up home. We keep them close and it is a love affair that goes back millennia. But why are roses such treasured flowers? Is it the combined power of fragrance and beauty?

Natural Perfume

The scent of a rose is so familiar, so comforting – almost as though its intoxicating elements are embedded in our subconscious. Who among us does not go to smell a rose bloom almost instinctively when we see one in a garden or as part of a bouquet? Why does it matter so much to us whether it is perfumed or not?

From the earliest writings and in art, man has demonstrated that the rose is an inspiration, held in high regard and has used it to symbolize a range of emotions, qualities and values. Roses feature in all the world's major religious texts and are intertwined with myths, legends and fairy tales. The Greek goddess Aphrodite was

Did You Know?

When the Jamestown settlers first arrived in America at Virginia Beach, Captain John Smith recorded that the Native Americans were growing many wild roses around their dwellings for pleasure, though it is known that they also used them for medicines, food and for spiritual reasons.

strongly linked to the rose and when the Romans renamed her Venus, the rose became the foremost symbol of love.

▶ **Simplicity and purity:** There is a mathematical simplicity to the white wild rose, with its five-petalled blooms and perfectly placed sepals (bud casings).

▶ **Love and romance:** Rose petals are velvety soft and the perfume seductive. Even in pure white roses, there is often a tinge or 'blush' of pink. And the shape of a rose in bud or unfolding is exquisitely beautiful. At the heart is a starry burst of golden stamens, a treasure to be discovered within a many-petalled bloom.

▶ **Ephemeral love:** Roses, like all flowers, eventually fade, but the rose seems to some to represent a poetic journey. Its development mirrors the stages of love, from the freshness and hope of a new affair still in bud, to a full-blown romance. Eventually petals fall or 'shatter' and the rose love story ends.

The rose is an emblem of Aphrodite, goddess of love

Did You Know?

One Greek legend of the red rose's creation tells of Aphrodite running to the side of her wounded lover, Adonis. In her haste, she scratched her foot on a white rose, turning it red with her blood.

▶ **Thorns:** The truth that this beautiful flower invariably has thorns is symbolic of the pain sometimes experienced when in love and the heartbreak of a love lost.

Ancient Records

The earliest depiction of a rose can be clearly seen on the edge of the bluebird fresco in the sixteenth-century-BC Minoan palace of Knossos, Crete. Mesopotamian cuneiform tablets indicate roses were important to humans going back 5,000 years, when it is also believed roses were being used in China. One tablet tells of Sargon I, King of Akkadia (2684–2630 BC) bringing rose saplings back from a military campaign to a country beyond the River Tigris, believed to be modern-day Turkey.

Did You Know?

Roses are depicted on the walls of a tomb of an Egyptian pharaoh, who died in the fourteenth century BC. Much later, in a second-century-AD tomb, a funeral wreath made from pink roses was discovered. When the petals were put in water, they returned to almost perfect condition.

Highly Prized

Ancient Assyrian tablets do not identify specific rose species grown or harvested at the time, but do record the fragrance of roses and the making and uses of rose water, probably from the fragrant *Rosa gallica, R. moschata* and a hybrid of at least three species (presumed resulting from man's activities), known as the Damask rose. Rose petals were heated up in water to produce small amounts of this high-value perfumed liquid.

Romans and the Rose

The Greeks and Romans cultivated forms of Rosa gallica widely, using them for perfumes, medicines, decorations, celebrations and votive offerings. It is interesting to see how many connections to the use of roses in modern-day life there are.

▶ **Walking on roses:** Wealthy Romans had their villa floors strewn with fragrant rose petals.

▶ **Secret elixir:** Cosmetic rose products were almost a currency amongst wealthy Roman women, who believed that the various health and beauty treatments could restore their beauty.

▶ **Roses and wine:** Rose petals were mixed with wine in an effort to stave off intoxication.

▶ **Hail the conquering heroes!** Rose petal confetti was showered over returning soldiers from overhanging balconies.

▶ **Wedding day:** Newlyweds wore rose headdresses.

Did You Know?

In Roman times, rose decorations were displayed above the heads of banqueters as a reminder to keep secret anything that was seen or done, and today the legal term *sub rosa*, refers to secrecy or confidentiality.

Emperor Nero's Rose Avalanche

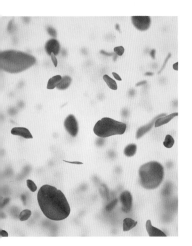

The first-century AD Roman Emperor Nero, known for his excesses, is reputed to have suspended vast quantities of rose petals over the heads of his guests at a banquet, releasing them as a surprise. Whether this was pure indulgence or a more sinister act of suffocating his guests is unknown. The painting by Sir Lawrence Alma-Tadema called *The Roses of Heliogabalus* depicts a similar Roman legend. Roses were out of season in Britain and so he had petals shipped over from the South of France each week.

Did You Know?

In one of the many tales of Cleopatra, a renowned seductress, it is reported that she had her chambers filled with rose petals, so that every time Mark Antony smelled or saw roses, he would think of her.

Roman Gardens

Large rose gardens for public use were established to the south of Rome and elsewhere in the Roman Empire. Before the fall of Rome in 476 AD, it is thought that there were in the region of 2,000 of these rose parks. Most wealthy households would have had their own private rose gardens.

24

The Route to the Modern Rose

Research looking at rose-decorated pottery and porcelain, frescos, paintings and furniture suggests that the roses cultivated in China about a thousand years ago had some of the characteristics of modern-day roses, including the shape and, most significantly, repeat flowering. Varieties were being selected and enhanced by breeding around 600 years ago, but it was not until the late eighteenth century that Chinese roses finally made their way to Europe, their arrival causing a sea change in breeding.

Did You Know?

The collections at Sangerhausen in Germany and the Roseraie de L'Haÿ near Paris would later far surpass Empress Josephine's in number and, unlike Malmaison back in Josephine's time, were entirely devoted to roses.

Ancient China

It is estimated that in some form or other, China has been utilizing or growing roses for around 5,000 years. This relationship began with wild species and early hybrids, which were widely used for medicines. Around 500 BC Confucius wrote of the roses grown in the Imperial Palace Gardens and that the emperor's library had more than a hundred books on roses.

French Rose Breeding

In 1799, Napoleon Bonaparte's wife, Empress Josephine, purchased Châteaux de Malmaison as a country retreat on the outskirts of Paris. Here, she kept her diverse collections of exotic animals and plants. The rose was one of her passions and between 1804 and 1814, she built the largest collection of roses in the world, comprising about 250 species and varieties.

A Melting Pot of Roses

Josephine's rose collection, many grown in pots, brought together rose species, hybrids, varieties and cultivars from all over the world, including many, surprisingly, purchased from the British nursery Kennedy and Lee. These were given safe passage despite the French naval blockade. Amongst these was a group of remontant (repeat-blooming) China roses, including *Rosa* 'Parson's Pink China' (*R.* x *odorata* 'Pallida') and *R.* 'Hume's Blush' (*R.* x *odorata* 'Odorata').

An Explosion of New Varieties

Josephine's unique collection at Malmaison encouraged French rose breeders to hybridize new varieties, and eventually, this resulted in the creation of the first modern rose. Josephine's head gardener, André du Pont, himself developed 200 new rose varieties.

The rose continues to develop today – new cultivars are continually sent for evaluation to the International Rose Test Garden in Washington Park, Portland, Oregon

The Perfumes of the Rose

Rose oil, or attar of roses, is an incredibly precious product, blended to make some of the finest perfumes. It is used as an active ingredient and fragrance for cosmetics, skin and hair products, and is a component of a variety of medical treatments. In some parts of the world, it is also used in religious ceremonies.

Did You Know?

Freshly picked petals of *Rosa gallica*, *R. × damascena* and *R. × centifolia* are the main sources used in oil production. It takes about 10,000 roses to make 5 ml (⅛ fl oz) of rose oil or, looking at it another way, 113 kg (250 lb) of petals makes just 30 ml (30 fl oz) of oil. Petals are picked very early in the morning, when they are still moist with dew, and have to be processed within 24 hours of harvest.

Oil Production

Rose oil is steam-distilled from rose petals heated in water, a process developed in medieval Iran. Rose oil was once produced in India and countries of the former Persian and Ottoman empires and some still goes on in these regions. Today, the main manufacturing countries are Bulgaria, the chief producer, Turkey and Morocco. Modern rose oil is distilled or solvent extracted. The less concentrated rose water is largely a by-product of distillation.

Turkish Delights

All kinds of rose-water-flavoured sweetmeats come from Turkey and the Middle East. Turkish delight actually covers a range of sweets, the most famous of which to Western eyes are coloured a delicate pink, flavoured with rose petals and rose water, and dusted with fine sugar. But this sweetmeat also comes flavoured with orange-flower water, mint and various spices. There are numerous rose-water-flavoured desserts, including rose ice cream as well as ground rose-petal jam.

The Enduring Appeal of Roses

Roses are still incredibly popular flowers for use at weddings and the trend is currently for many-petalled blooms and for roses with an old rose look. More trend-setting varieties are always being developed and a new pink, star-shaped double rose called *Rosa* 'Miyabi' has recently been introduced for the floristry industry by Japanese breeder Wabara.

A Dozen Red Roses

It has been estimated that a staggering 224 million roses are grown for Valentine's Day, a large percentage of which are red, but pink is also popular. Roses for the cut-flower industry are grown all over the world, and long-stemmed roses popular in certain countries like Russia are produced in places like Ecuador and Kenya, where the climate and conditions suit.

What's in a Name?

Cultivar names play a large part in the fascination we have for roses and add to their appeal. The names of historic and heritage roses can be so tantalizing and romantic-sounding, especially as many of them are French, that a rose will be purchased almost regardless of its horticultural qualities. Rose identification can be confusing, as many older varieties are known by several different names.

Powerful People

In the nineteenth century, roses were often named after members of Europe's ruling elite. The names are a veritable who's who of high society at the time. Figures from the aristocracy, from the Church, from government and the military were popular sources.

Rosa 'Diana, Princess of Wales' will be an ever-popular rose

English Roses

Rose breeder David Austin evokes a sense of history through his choice of names. These are often characters gathered from literature, poets, playwrights and authors, as well as famous gardens and gardeners of old. The success or failure of a rose is hugely dependent on the popularity of its chosen name, and rose producers today often reference popular culture, name them after media stars or use names that resonate with buyers looking for something to mark a special date.

Checklist

▶ **A long association:** Man has been using roses for medicine, food, perfume and in spiritual practices for more than 5,000 years.

▶ **Myths and legends:** Greek and Roman mythology is littered with references to roses.

▶ **First painting:** The oldest image of a rose was discovered at the sixteenth-century-BC Palace of Knossos, Crete.

▶ **Early written records:** Mesopotamian cuneiform tablets include an account of Sargon, King of Akkadia (2684–2630 BC) bringing rose saplings back from a military campaign.

▶ **China:** This country has one of the longest histories of rose-growing and hybridization. In 500 BC, Confucius wrote of roses in the imperial gardens and of the emperor's library of over 100 books on roses.

▶ **Symbolism:** The rose is an inspiration for philosophers, writers, poets and artists.

▶ **Religious and spiritual:** All the world's major religions have references to the rose.

▶ **Love token:** The rose is the foremost expression of love, a favourite at weddings and on Valentine's Day.

▶ **Josephine's obsession:** The Empress Josephine's rose collection (1804–14) at Château de Malmaison brought together species and varieties from around the world, sparking an explosion in rose breeding.

A Gallery

of Roses

Evolution of the Garden Rose

Domestic roses evolved from the wild rose

The origins of the rose have been traced to central Asia, an estimated 60 to 70 million years ago. These early roses evolved and spread throughout much of Asia and Europe across ancient land bridges to colonize North America. Today, more than 200 wild rose species remain in temperate regions of the northern hemisphere, but only around a third of these are grown in gardens and just seven have been used in the breeding of garden varieties. Rose hybrids and cultivars now number in their thousands, with worldwide distribution.

Rose Groupings

Roses are grouped into three broad categories – Wild roses, Old Garden roses and Modern roses – within which there are sub-categories based on breeding lines and common characteristics. Rose species and their naturally occurring varieties hybridize freely. The breeding of garden roses has been greatly assisted by this and the fact that the genetic characteristics of natural varieties as well as man-made cultivars can also be relatively easily blended.

Rosa 'Felicia' is a Hybrid Musk rose, a group that is often classified under Old Garden roses

Selection Process

Throughout the long history of rose cultivation, gardeners have been crossing roses to select for certain characteristics. Among the great many failures of the seedlings grown to flowering size, there will be one or two that show promise. Further growing trials confirm whether these are garden-worthy. Manipulated features include:

Rosa 'Chicago Peace' is a 'sport' of the famous 'Peace' rose

- ▶ Flower form, shape and size
- ▶ Colour
- ▶ Habit (shape and appearance) and size of the plant
- ▶ Length of flowering
- ▶ Fragrance
- ▶ Disease resistance
- ▶ Cold, heat and humidity tolerance

Around the World

Roses have always been highly prized, especially for their perfume, and have been distributed along the ancient trade routes, across seas and oceans. Migrants would carry rose cuttings from their former homes, and early North American settlers famously took plants and herbs with them from the old country. Roses travelling by ship to Australia and New Zealand would have had a tough time surviving the long voyage and wide temperature variations. The tough Scots or Burnet rose (*Rosa spinosissima*) and other pimpinellifolia types were among those that made it through.

Did You Know?

Roses can produce 'sports' (parts of the plant that spontaneously appear and are completely different in appearance and character). These can then be propagated vegetatively (for example, from cuttings). Examples include the pink-shaded 'Chicago Peace', a sport of the famous 'Peace' rose, and 'Climbing Iceberg', a climbing sport from the original pure white Floribunda rose of the same name.

Wild Roses

The 'species roses' (or wild roses) are mostly single-flowered with five petals, shaded white, pink or red (though there are yellow exceptions) and many also carry heavy crops of hips, an important resource for wildlife. They typically form dense, impenetrable mounds or thickets, though some scramble up rock faces or into trees. Depending on their geographic origins, they are generally hardy and disease-resistant.

Varied Habitats

Rose species are found growing in wildly differing conditions of climate and soil type. At least one is a desert dweller, hugging the ground to conserve moisture. Some are coastal, coping with saline soils, salt spray or shifting sand dunes. Many live in semi-woodland or in scrub, and some are prairie or steppe dwellers. Still others grow at high altitudes or relatively high latitudes and are extremely tolerant of cold, while a few roses have evolved in warm, temperate climates.

Did You Know?

Wild roses can flourish at a much faster rate when growing in warmer climates than they are used to. This sometimes leads to problems when a foreign species is introduced or escapes from garden cultivation. Certain species are now classified as invasive, such as *Rosa multiflora* in the US.

Wild Roses of Asia

A great many of the wild roses from Asia are highly significant in the breeding of the cultivated roses we enjoy today. Others are popular garden plants in their own right, especially in the form of selected varieties.

▶ *Rosa banksiae*: Lady Banks' rose is a double white Rambler, or soft yellow in the form *R. b.* 'Lutea'. Both flower mid- to late spring, have glossy leaves and prefer a sheltered location. China.

▶ *R. chinensis*: This pink species from Southwest China was interbred with *R. gigantea* to form *R. × odorata* and cultivars including the enchanting 'Mutabilis'. Modern roses derive their repeat-blooming trait from *R. chinensis*.

R. banksiae

▶ *R. foetida*: This introduction from the Caucasus Mountains in Georgia, formerly within the Persian Empire, provided the all-important yellow colour for Modern roses. Early forms in European gardens were variously called the Austrian copper rose (*R. foetida* 'Bicolor'), Persian yellow rose or Persian double. Unfortunately, it also introduced the fungal disease black spot.

R. × odorata 'Mutabilis', derived from *R. chinensis*

R. laevigata

▶ *R. laevigata*: The Cherokee rose is from Southeast Asia and this white-flowered Rambler thrives in warmer climates. It is classed as invasive in parts of the US, but is the state flower of Georgia.

▶ *R. lucieae* (formerly *R. wichurana*): Originally from Japan, the memorial rose is so called because it was widely planted in cemeteries in the twentieth century. It makes virtually evergreen ground cover with a mass of single cream-tinged pink blooms in summer followed by dark red hips. Introduced to the US, it grows wild having escaped from gardens, sometimes marking old habitation sites.

R. foetida

37

R. moschata

R. moyesii

R. multiflora

▶ *R. moschata*: The musk rose is a late-summer-flowering white, single or double Rambler known since ancient times and certainly in garden cultivation since the sixteenth century. Significant in the breeding of Damask and Noisette roses, it is highly rated for its unusually long flowering period and strong fragrance. It was mentioned in Shakespeare's *A Midsummer Night's Dream*.

▶ *R. moyesii*: This blood-red to pink species from Western China has flask- or flagon-shaped hips and has been used in rose breeding. *Rosa* 'Geranium' is a popular summer-flowering hybrid, compact with red single blooms, dainty foliage and large scarlet hips.

▶ *R. multiflora*: Also referred to as the Polyantha rose, this native of China, Japan and Korea is a scrambling shrub. Its single white or pink blooms appear in clusters during early summer, followed by red-purple hips. It is used as rootstock for grafted rose cultivars and is the parent of the Polyantha and Floribunda roses.

R. lucieae

Did You Know?

Rosa lucieae was used in the breeding of a number of famous Ramblers and climbers, including the deep pink double 'Dorothy Perkins' and 'Albéric Barbier' with double summer blooms, creamy and yellow-tinged in bud. The double blooms of 'Albertine', salmon to light pink, are richly fragrant. 'New Dawn' (pale-flesh pink, semi-double) is a repeat-flowering climber with glossy foliage.

Did You Know?

Recent breeding using *Rosa persica* (the red dot rose) has introduced a range of striking new cultivars with single or double blooms, each with a dark eye. These include the Babylon Eyes® series (Sweet Spot® in the US); the Eyeconic® series, bred for hot, dry climates like California; and two individuals: 'For Your Eyes Only' (fragrant single orange-pink with maroon blotch) and 'Eyes for You' (highly fragrant semi-double pale lilac with dark centres).

R. sericea subsp. *omeiensis* f. *pteracantha*

▶ **R. persica**: This extraordinary rose with leathery, glaucous leaves is found in steppes and deserts from Afghanistan and Iran to western Siberia. The flat blooms are yellow with a red eye.

▶ **R. rugosa**: A coastal species from China, Japan, Korea and Siberia, surviving even on sand dunes, it has long been cultivated and used for fragrant potpourri and in Chinese medicine. Large, deep pink blooms develop into tomato-shaped hips. *Rugosa* refers to the wrinkled leaves. Given good drainage, this and the Rugosa hybrids such as the double, highly scented 'Hansa' are trouble-free. *See also* page 61.

▶ **R. sericea** subsp. *omeiensis* f. *pteracantha*: The aptly named 'winged thorn rose' is best appreciated in winter, when the large translucent red thorns are backlit by low sun. It comes from Western China and is highly unusual, having only four white petals instead of the usual five.

R. persica

R. 'For Your Eyes Only'

R. rugosa

39

R. xanthina

▶ *R. xanthina*: The Manchu rose from China, Korea and Mongolia is another rare yellow. In the commonly grown form 'Canary Bird', which has dainty foliage, the blooms are large and flat, festooning the shrub's arching stems in mid- to late spring.

Wild Roses of Europe

Though few wild European roses were involved in the development of today's roses, *Rosa canina* and *R. arvensis* brought about the resilient Albas. Several make fine garden plants in their own right and some offer huge benefits to wildlife, providing food and habitat for bees, birds and mammals.

R. arvensis

▶ *Rosa arvensis*: The field rose is a white blooming shrub that lives in hedgerows and woodlands through Europe, flowering once in late spring or early summer. Hips for birds follow.

▶ *R. canina*: The dog rose has a wide range across Europe, but also occurs naturally in North West Africa and across to Western Asia. The pretty white-shading-to-pink blooms festoon hedges and woodland byways in

R. canina hips

Did You Know?

During the Second World War, Britain's Ministry of Food urged people to gather hedgerow harvests and to pick wild and cultivated rose hips, rich in vitamin C, for rose hip syrup. The hips were collected in local areas and processed commercially, ready to be sold in shops. Leaflets explained that: 'A teaspoonful of rose hip syrup a day will supply half the vitamin C needs of a child.'

40

early summer. In autumn, the red hips appear and these have a wide variety of uses, both culinary and medicinal. Dog rose is also used commercially for budding roses.

R. glauca

▶ **R. glauca**: The red-leafed rose hails from the mountains of Central and Southern Europe and is naturalized further north. Widely included in gardens for its foliage effect (a glaucous purple), the mid-summer blooms with vivid pink and white pointed petals are a bonus. Glossy red fruits follow. Suitable for hedging.

▶ **R. rubiginosa**: The aptly named sweet briar, or, as Shakespeare called it, eglantine, has apple-scented foliage that smells heavenly after summer rain. It can be found across Europe and Western Asia. The pink blooms are also highly fragrant.

R. rubiginosa

R. spinosissima

▶ **R. spinosissima**: The Scots or Burnet rose, formerly *R. pimpinellifolia*, has creamy white single blooms lasting around a month on a low, suckering shrub (*see R. carolina*, page 42) with ferny foliage. The glossy black hips are spherical. Plants are extremely tough and able to grow on poor soils. By 1840, there were known to be around 500 cultivars of Scots rose. A few still commercially available include:

R. s. 'Andrewsii': Double pink
R. s. double, white-flowered: As its name imples.
R. s. 'Mary, Queen of Scots': Single two-tone lilac pink
R. s. 'William III': Magenta pink semi-double

41

R. setigera

R. acicularis

Wild Roses of North America

Some of the roses in this group have a wide distribution, including the prairie rose *Rosa arkansana* with its showy globular red hips, and the fragrant pink *R. setigera*. A few stand out for having rich autumn colouring. North American species can be extremely cold-hardy and some are tolerant of sea spray. Others include:

▶ **Rosa acicularis**: The prickly wild rose bears attractive flask-shaped red hips and has vibrant autumn leaf colour.

▶ **R. carolina**: The pasture rose is a suckering shrub (it sends up new stems from below ground, increasing its spread), forming low thickets. Its fragrant pink blooms show in early summer and are followed by attractive hips. Despite needing drainage, it can be found growing on stream banks.

▶ **R. nutkana**: The Nootka rose bears spicy-scented pinky lavender flowers in early summer and has long-lasting round hips. It grows in coastal locations, forest and stream margins in western North America and Alaska. It is also used in Native American medicine.

R. carolina

R. nutkana

42

Did You Know?

The Yellow Rose of Texas, *Rosa* 'Harison's Yellow' or the Oregon Trail rose, is thought to be a hybrid between the yellow *Rosa foetida* and white Scots rose (*R. spinosissima*). The plant is naturalized along the Oregon Trail and pops up at the sites of abandoned homes in the Western United States. It thrives on poor soil, and suckers, making thickets covered in semi-double yellow blooms for several weeks in spring. This is the rose mentioned in the Civil War song 'The Yellow Rose of Texas'.

R. 'Harison's Yellow'

▶ *R. stellata* var. *mirifica*: This species goes under several names, including the Sacramento rose and gooseberry rose. It has large blooms of deep pink from late spring into early summer.

▶ *R. virginiana*: The American wild rose or shining leaf rose bears small pink flowers in summer, good fruits and has colourful autumn tints. It grows along the Eastern Seaboard and is tolerant of saline soils but also makes a good garden shrub. *R. v.* 'Plena', properly known as *R.* 'Rose d'Amour', has double pink blooms.

R. virginiana

R. woodsii

▶ *R. woodsii*: The western wild rose is a cold-hardy native found across Canada and Alaska, and has relatively large single pink fragrant blooms.

43

Old Garden Roses

This is a diverse group, sometimes also known as heritage, historic or heirloom roses, covering roses bred before the advent of the first Hybrid Tea rose in 1867. These roses often have a very high petal count and instantly recognizable bloom shapes – shapes reimagined in several Modern Shrub roses bred to have a vintage look. The strong 'old rose' fragrance of many is irresistible. They typically bloom once between late spring and summer, though some are remontant (flower more than once).

R. 'Lady of the Mist', an heirloom rose

Damask

These highly fragrant roses, some of the oldest in cultivation, are thought to have been developed from hybrids formed in ancient times between *Rosa moschata*, *R. gallica*, *R. fedtschenkoana* and others, not found growing together naturally. There are two types: the summer Damask, blooming once in summer, and the autumn Damask, which has a second, later flush. Colours range from white to deep pink.

44

Did You Know?

Legend has it that the Damask rose was brought from Syria to France by the knight Robert de Brie when he was returning from the Crusades, though scientists think the original Damasks came from Persia.

R. × damascena var. *versicolor*

▶ *Rosa × damascena* var. *semperflorens*: One of the twice-flowering autumn Damask roses, this semi-double pink rose goes under the names Four Seasons or Quatre Saisons rose and Rose of Castille. Its habit is open, upright to arching.

▶ *R. × d.* var. *versicolor*: Known as the York and Lancaster rose, this is more of a collector's item, with variable pale pink and white stripes or broader pink shading.

▶ Hebe's Lip: One of the Damask hybrids crossed with the sweet briar (*R. rubiginosa*), it is a semi-double white with cupped blooms (that is, longer outer petals curving slightly inwards) and a central boss of golden stamens. Myrrh fragrance.

▶ Ispahan: Named after the ancient Persian capital, these double mid-pink roses are one of the earlier and longest flowering.

R. × damascena var. *semperflorens*

R. 'Hebe's Lip'

R. 'Ispahan'

45

R. 'La Ville de Bruxelles'

▶ **La Ville de Bruxelles:** This is an upright shrub with fully double and quartered pink blooms that are slightly cupped. Height to 1.5 m (5 ft).

▶ **Madame Hardy:** A large spreading shrub, this bears luxuriantly double, quartered blooms of white with a tiny green eye.

R. 'Madame Hardy'

Gallica

Dating back to the twelfth century, these roses were grown for their medicinal properties as well as their intense perfume. The fragrant petals of *Rosa gallica* var. *officinalis* were once produced in vast quantities around the French town of Provins. Like the Albas, they are once-blooming (once-flowering, non-remontant), tolerant of cold and a little shade, though they thrive in sun. The summer flowers come in rich shades of reds and purples as well as pinks. Some are striped. Compact shrubs around 1.2 m (4 ft), often with few thorns.

R. gallica 'Versicolor'
(syn. Rosa mundi)

▶ **R. g. var. officinalis:** The apothecary's rose has a long history as a medicinal plant and is thought to be the Red Rose of Lancaster. Its blooms are semi-double fuchsia pink with a boss of golden stamens.

▶ **R. g. 'Versicolor':** The rosa mundi is a deep-pink-and-white-striped sport of the apothecary's rose and is similarly historic. A favourite in herb gardens.

R. gallica var. *officinalis*

46

R. 'Tuscany Superb'

▶ **Charles de Mills:** This cultivar's flattened fully double flowers are shaded deep carmine red and purple. It makes an easy-care, low, informal hedge.

▶ **Tuscany Superb:** The velvety deep purple-red petals of this semi-double fragrant shrub invite touch. The glimpse of golden stamens adds to the sensuous appeal.

R. 'Charles de Mills'

▶ **Cardinal de Richelieu:** This striking shrub is a little taller than most Gallicas and though not as richly fragrant as some, the flowers have a moody burgundy-purple enchantment. The large double blooms form into globe shapes as they mature.

R. alba 'Alba Semiplena'

Alba

R. 'Cardinal de Richelieu'

Alba hybrids have the European *Rosa arvensis* and *R. × alba* (a hybrid of *R. gallica* and the dog rose, *R. canina*) in their mix. They are hardy and disease-free as well as being moderately shade tolerant. Hybrids can sometimes be traced back to 1400 or even earlier. They make tall bushy plants with blue- or grey-green foliage. The white or pale pink headily fragrant flowers appear in abundance in late spring or early summer.

▶ *Rosa × alba* **'Alba Semiplena':** This is the White Rose of York, a semi-double opening almost flat with a boss of yellow stamens.

47

R. 'Königin von Dänemark'

R. 'Maiden's Blush'

R. × centifolia

▶ **Königin von Dänemark:** The glaucous foliage makes the perfect foil for the fully double pink blooms.

▶ **Madame Plantier:** The double white blooms are pink in bud to pretty effect. Well clothed in foliage, this Alba hybrid can also be grown as a climber.

▶ **Maiden's Blush:** This old cultivar is tall and arching and could be used as a climber for a shady north wall. The fully double palest pink blooms are cream in bud.

R. 'Madame Plantier'

Centifolia

Also known as Provence roses due to their association with the perfume industry (and also, rather unflatteringly, as cabbage roses), these sun-loving roses have their origins in *Rosa × centifolia*, a seventeenth-century Dutch hybrid related to the famously fragrant Damask roses. The flower heads are so packed with petals they sometimes nod under the weight. The white or pink shaded blooms are intensely fragrant and are produced once in early summer. Prone to disease.

▶ *Rosa × centifolia*: This bright mid-pink rose is a lax shrub with grey-green foliage. Long stems carry the double, cupped and richly fragrant blooms.

48

▶ *R. × c.* **'Cristata':** The crested cabbage rose demonstrates a trait of Centifolias in forming mutations. In this case, the green bud casings or sepals each have a mossy crest. Blooms are cupped pink doubles.

R. × centifolia 'Cristata'

R. × centifolia 'De Meaux'

▶ *R. × c.* **'De Meaux':** This dwarf, lightly scented shrub dates from 1785. It has dainty foliage and miniature mid-pink fully double blooms that are quartered. Centifolias were the origins of the first truly miniature roses.

▶ *R. × c.* **'Unique Panachée':** An exquisite old rose with fully double white quartered blooms stained with pink produced over a long period.

▶ **Paul Ricault:** A cross with a Hybrid Perpetual rose, this deep, rich, pink-flowered shrub has plentiful blooms that hang gracefully from the plant. The flowers are fully double and quartered with a pervasive fragrance.

▶ **Petite de Hollande:** This compact shrub bears a multitude of small double pink blooms that have a sweet fragrance.

R. × centifolia 'Unique Panachée'

Portland Roses

These have autumn Damask and Gallica roses in their breeding and are named after the Duchess of Portland. Around 1775, a rose was sent to her from Italy, known as the Scarlet Four Seasons Rose, from which all the Portland roses were developed. These suckering shrubs are compact and repeat-flowering, although the main season is summer. The blooms have very little stem and the foliage seems to crowd around them.

49

R. 'De Resht'

R. 'Madame Boll'

R. 'Marchesa
Boccella'

50

▶ **De Resht:** This fragrant hybrid makes a small bush with rounded deep fuchsia blooms packed with petals. When healthy, it repeats well. From 1840.

▶ **Portlandica:** Also known as *R.* 'Duchess of Portland', this compact rose bears cerise-red semi-double blooms with a central boss of golden stamens. Susceptible to disease.

▶ **Madame Boll:** Sometimes sold as 'Comte de Chambord', this has headily fragrant, fully double ball-shaped blooms of rich rose pink fading to pale pink as they open flatter. It repeats well and has excellent disease resistance. From 1860.

▶ **Marchesa Boccella:** This sumptuous rose, sometimes confused with 'Jacques Cartier', has fragrant fully double quartered blooms of pink on stems to 1.2 m (4 ft). May suffer fungal diseases.

▶ **Rose du Roi:** A parent of the Hybrid Perpetual roses, this fragrant compact rose bears fully double magenta red blooms with purple shading. Good repeating and disease resistance. From 1815.

R. 'Portlandica' (syn. 'Duchess of Portland')

R. 'Rose du Roi'

Bourbon

Thought to be derived from a natural cross between the autumn Damask and the 'Old Blush China' rose (*Rosa* × *odorata* 'Pallida'), they were introduced to France in the 1820s. Their opulent blooms in shades of pink, white or red appear in flushes. Many have an intense fragrance. Bourbons tend to have very few thorns, purple-tinged stems and light green, glossy, if somewhat disease-prone, foliage. Often narrow and upright, they lend themselves to be trained as short climbers. Not for cold climates.

R. 'Madame Isaac Péreire'

▶ **Madame Isaac Péreire:** A widely available climbing Bourbon, with double raspberry pink quartered blooms and rich fragrance, blooming summer and autumn.

▶ **Honorine de Brabant:** A striped form with cupped double blooms in pink-streaked purple and magenta. Shade-tolerant and repeats well, with later flowers often improved.

R. 'Honorine de Brabant'

▶ **Louise Odier:** A vigorous rose well clothed in foliage and unusually thorny. The cupped, bright lilac-pink blooms open flatter to petal-packed circles.

R. 'Louise Odier'

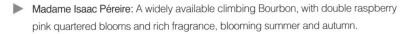

Did You Know?

These roses get their name from the island where they originated in the Indian Ocean off the coast of Madagascar. Formerly Île Bourbon, it is now known as Réunion.

51

R. 'Madame Pierre Oger'

R. 'Souvenir de la Malmaison'

▶ **Madame Pierre Oger:** The ball-shaped silvery pink blooms open from red-tinged buds that stain the outer petals carmine. Susceptible to black spot.

▶ **Reine Victoria:** A repeat-flowering deep lilac pink with cupped, richly fragrant blooms.

▶ **Souvenir de la Malmaison:** Named after Empress Josephine's famous rose collection, this old cultivar has palest pink quartered double blooms opening flat. Irregular repeats and best in a dry summer, avoiding rain damage to the blooms. Climber.

▶ **Zéphirine Drouhin:** A climber with semi-double rich cerise-pink blooms in abundance through summer into autumn. Strong fragrance. May be grown on a shady north wall. Needs rich moisture-retentive soil to reduce mildew.

R. 'Reine Victoria'

R. 'Zéphirine Drouhin'

China

A group of China roses arrived in Europe from East Asia during the late eighteenth and early nineteenth centuries. They carried with them the genes for developing the Modern rose. The hybrids were mostly fragrant and small, and the unfurling buds opened in classic Hybrid Tea rose fashion. Multiple colours suddenly became available and plants were repeat-blooming well into autumn. Chinas are rather tender, needing winter protection.

▶ *R. × odorata* 'Hume's Blush Tea-scented China': This compact shrub carries loosely double blush-pink blooms with a tea fragrance. The outer petals are stained darker pink.

▶ *R. × o.* 'Mutabilis': This is an extraordinary rose with purple-flushed stems and abundant single blooms with twisted petals, giving a butterfly effect. The flame buds open to coppery yellow and transform through deeper pink shades. Grow as a shrub or short climber. Best in a protected position.

R. × odorata 'Hume's Blush Tea-scented China'

R. 'Cramoisi Supérieur'

▶ *R. × o.* 'Pallida': One of the 'stud' Chinas that gave rise to the first of the modern Hybrid Teas, this was originally called *R.* 'Old Blush China' or *R.* 'Parson's Pink China'. The double pink, fragrant blooms with darker shading are produced on upright shrubs through summer into autumn.

▶ Cramoisi Supérieur: This cupped, bright crimson flowered rose also goes by the names 'Agrippina', 'Lady Brisbane' or the Bermuda rose. Its lightly perfumed blooms, white flecked at the centre, are produced over a long period in warm climates. Prone to black spot.

R. x odorata 'Mutabilis'

R. × odorata 'Pallida' (syn. *R.* 'Old Blush China' and R. 'Parson's Pink China')

▶ Louis Philippe: A short-growing shrub, this rose has small, cupped double blooms of deep crimson red, but little fragrance.

R. 'Louis Philippe'

53

Tea Roses

When China roses were introduced to Europe in the late 1700s along with a yellow flowered climber from Asia (*R. grandiflora*), early hybrids inherited their repeat blooming ability but were not particularly hardy or robust. Breeders, mainly in France, began crossing them with other roses, particularly Bourbons. The resultant 'Tea' roses had strong stems and large fragrant blooms with sharply conical buds. On opening, the edges of the petals roll back to form points. They come in a wide colour range, repeat well and are disease resistant but lack hardiness.

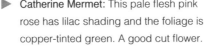

R. 'Catherine Mermet'

▶ **Catherine Mermet:** This pale flesh pink rose has lilac shading and the foliage is copper-tinted green. A good cut flower.

▶ **Duchesse de Brabant:** With very few thorns, this compact, double, light pink rose is a delight in pots on the terrace.

▶ **Général Schablikine:** The long buds open to coppery pink petals with darker red shading. The heads are nodding and the shrub can be used as an informal hedge.

R. 'Duchesse de Brabant'

▶ **Gloire de Dijon:** A well-known Climbing Tea rose, to 5.5 m (18 ft), this buff yellow double has a fruity fragrance.

Did You Know?

Early settlers on the island of Bermuda brought with them old roses from their homelands. Many lost their original names and provenance but were found still thriving in the tough Caribbean climate. They are collectively known as the Bermuda Mystery Roses, often named after the owners of the gardens in which they were rediscovered.

R. 'Gloire de Dijon'

R. 'Climbing Lady Hillingdon'

▶ **Climbing Lady Hillingdon:** The well-formed heads of this yellow, large-flowered climber hang down from the branches, emitting a strong fragrance. More vigorous than *R.* 'Gloire de Dijon'.

▶ **Maman Cochet:** This rose, with large, double blooms and curled-back petals, is a pale pink with deep pinky-red shading and yellow centres. Very few thorns.

▶ **Safrano:** A pale yellow to apricot semi-double, the large-flowered *R.* 'Safrano' has almost smooth stems, and new foliage growth is purple-red tinted, making a fine contrast with the blooms.

R. 'Maman Cochet'

R. 'Céline Forestier'

Noisette

Noisettes repeat well, and are generally fragrant with clusters of blooms on tall, bushy plants. Due to crossings of the original Noisettes with Tea roses gaining a wider range of pastels, the hardiness of later hybrids suffered.

▶ **Céline Forestier:** This fully double primrose yellow rose with large, tea-scented blooms can be grown as a short climber or a free-standing shrub, given some support. It repeats well with deadheading. Tender (that is, not hardy), so best in a warm, sheltered position in colder regions.

55

R. 'Desprez à Fleur Jaune'

R. 'Madame Alfred Carrière'

R. 'Noisette Carnée'

▶ **Desprez à Fleur Jaune:** The double quartered blooms of this vigorous repeat-flowering climber are soft yellow shaded buff and apricot pink. Healthy foliage and a strong fruity fragrance.

▶ **Lamarque:** A climber or large cascading shrub given support, this bears white double blooms tinted soft yellow at the centre on long, arching stems. It is disease-resistant, repeat-flowering with a strong fragrance, but requires a very warm and sheltered spot.

R. 'Lamarque'

▶ **Madame Alfred Carrière:** A hardy climber to 7.5 m (25 ft) with very few thorns, it is repeat-blooming and ideal for a shady north wall. The loosely double flowers are creamy white, sometimes tinged palest pink, with a strong, sweet scent.

▶ **Maréchal Niel:** This deep yellow climbing rose has large Hybrid-Tea-shaped blooms that hang down from lax stems and the tea fragrance is strong. Requires a warm climate, a highly sheltered position or cultivation under glass.

▶ **Noisette Carnée:** Short climber with repeating semi-double blooms in palest pink, cupped at first. Musk/clove scented. The first commercially available Noisette (formerly R. 'Blush Noisette').

R. 'Maréchal Niel'

Did You Know?

The original hybrid between *Rosa* × *odorata* 'Pallida' ('Parson's Pink China') and the musk (*R. moschata*) was raised by a South Carolina rice grower. *R.* 'Champneys Pink Cluster' was a vigorous climber with plentiful small pink blooms through summer into autumn. Samples were sent to his friend Philippe Noisette, who passed them on to brother Louis in Paris. It was Louis who introduced the re-named *R.* 'Blush Noisette' in 1817.

R. 'Rêve d'Or'

▶ **Rêve d'Or:** A tall climber to 5.5 m (18 ft), this buff yellow, almost fully double rose has pinky-apricot shading and fades with age. Attractive glossy foliage.

Hybrid Perpetual

In Victorian times, this class of roses was the most popular. They were developed by crossing and re-crossing most of the existing Old Garden rose groups with China and Tea roses. The name is somewhat misleading, as the cultivars often only flowered once in late spring or summer and then poorly after that. They came in a range of pinks, purples and reds, occasionally white, and produced large blooms that mostly had a strong fragrance.

R. 'Baroness Rothschild'

▶ **Baroness Rothschild:** This upright rose growing to 1.2 m (4 ft) with greyish green foliage and thorny stems bears large cupped light pink double blooms. Though there is only very light fragrance, it repeats reasonably well.

57

R. 'Ferdinand Pichard'

R. 'La Reine'

R. 'Paul Neyron'

R. 'Général Jacqueminot'

R. 'Reine des Violettes'

▶ **Ferdinand Pichard:** A bushy and thorny shrub with light green foliage, this bears double, globe-shaped blooms. There is an early main flush followed by smaller repeats. The blooms are palest pink striped with crimson and richly fragrant. Note: it is often listed as a Bourbon.

▶ **Général Jacqueminot:** This crimson-red beauty is the ancestor of most of today's red bush roses. The double blooms repeat well and have a rich fragrance.

▶ **La Reine:** Sumptuous double, quilted blooms in rosy lilac-pink fill the air with scent through summer into autumn. May be trained as a climber.

▶ **Paul Neyron:** Noted for its exceptionally large, fully double blooms in rich lilac-shaded pink, this cultivar unfortunately has quite weak growth, so needs support and protection from black spot.

▶ **Reine des Violettes:** Deservedly popular, this fully double-flowered shrub is virtually thornless. The fragrant blooms are a most unusual violet-mauve. It repeats well and has good disease resistance.

Hybrid Musk

Although technically developed too late to be included with the Old Garden roses, the Hybrid Musks have similar looks and requirements. Most of the breeding work was carried out by the Reverend Joseph Pemberton in Britain, early in the twentieth century. These roses have *Rosa multiflora* and the musk rose in their background. The clustered blooms have inherited the musk fragrance and repeat well. Shrubs are disease-resistant with lax stems and few thorns.

R. 'Ballerina'

▶ **Ballerina:** This popular landscaping rose is a Hybrid Musk/Polyantha cross. Apple-blossom-pink single blooms with white centres form in rounded clusters covering the low-mounded shrub through summer.

▶ **Buff Beauty:** Semi-double apricot buff blooms, with a good Tea rose scent, are carried on smooth stems. Grows to 1.2 m (4 ft).

▶ **Cornelia:** Clusters of double apricot blooms fading to peachy pink are freely produced on this large shrub with bronze-tinted leaves. 1.5 m (5 ft).

R. 'Buff Beauty'

▶ **Felicia:** Pointed buds open to loose, double, silvery-pink blooms, darker salmon pink towards the centre. May be used as a flowering hedge.

▶ **Penelope:** Clusters of palest pink, semi-double blooms adorn the arching stems through summer into autumn, followed by attractive hips.

R. 'Cornelia'

59

Moss

These curious roses, popular with the Victorians, are mostly Centifolia cultivars and hybrids. They take their name from the mossy growth covering their stems and flower buds. The blooms are fragrant and the 'moss' also gives off a woody or balsam-like scent when rubbed.

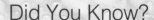

Did You Know?

After the death of the Reverend Joseph Pemberton, his assistant, Ann Bentall, went on to develop two roses of note, the Polyantha rose 'The Fairy' and the hybrid 'Ballerina'.

R. × centifolia 'Muscosa'

R. 'William Lobb'

▶ **R. × centifolia 'Muscosa':** Known as the common moss, this shrub rose has double pink cupped blooms that are strongly fragrant and repeat. The greenish brown mossy feathery growths on the buds are fascinating.

▶ **Général Kléber:** This once-flowering shrub has light pink semi-double blooms.

▶ **Mousseline:** A Damask-Portland hybrid, this is repeat-flowering with double pink cupped blooms and bushy upright growth to 1.5 m (5 ft). Also known as *R.* 'Alfred de Dalmas' (the autumn Damask rose).

▶ **William Lobb:** Almost fully double flowered, a deep purple-mauve overlaid with grey, this large, strongly perfumed shrub can be trained as a climber or allowed to spread in a semi-wild spot.

R. 'Général Kléber'

Hybrid Rugosa

Not officially Old Garden roses, these hybrids of *Rosa rugosa* (*see* page 39) are generally grouped with them. The healthy, rich green, wrinkled foliage makes a strong foil for the fragrant blooms, ranging from single to double, in white, pink, crimson, scarlet or purple. Most repeat well.

R. rugosa 'Alba'

▶ *Rosa rugosa* 'Alba': A pure white single-flowered shrub with large round red hips.

▶ Blanche Double de Coubert: This clean white double opens from pointed buds and is ideal as a fragrant hedge.

▶ Fru Dagmar Hastrup: This pretty hybrid has mid-pink single blooms followed by red, tomato-like hips.

R. 'Fru Dagmar Hastrup'

▶ Hansa: A vigorous, long-flowering Rugosa hybrid, 'Hansa' has deep purple-red double blooms. Excellent for hedging.

R. 'Roseraie de l'Haÿ'

▶ Roseraie de l'Haÿ: Flowering mid-summer to early autumn, this strong-growing hybrid has headily fragrant double blooms of rich magenta purple. Will tolerate a little shade.

▶ Sarah van Fleet: This large upright shrub bears pretty light to mid-pink, semi-double blooms that are slightly cupped on opening.

R. 'Hansa'

61

Modern Roses

This vast group contains any rose bred after 1867, but when most people think of a modern rose, they imagine the Hybrid Tea and Floribunda bush roses with their repeat-flowering (remontant) habit and wide array of colours. There are many shrub roses and climbers now that repeat reliably and the fragrance, health and hardiness accidentally bred out of many in the search for other attributes are being reintroduced.

R. 'Cécile Brünner'

Polyantha

These roses represent a stepping stone to creating the Floribunda rose and date back to 1875 when the white double 'La Pâquerette' was introduced in France. Polyanthas bear large clusters of tiny blooms, often double, in shades of pink, white or crimson. They repeat well, are low-maintenance and disease-free and ideal for container gardening or small plots.

R. 'Gruss an Aachen'

▶ **Cécile Brünner:** This dwarf Polyantha has fragrant palest pink double Tea-rose-type blooms and the flowers and foliage are miniature in form.

▶ **Gruss an Aachen:** A small, compact shrub, this bears fragrant pale pink double blooms fading to cream and has healthy foliage.

R. 'Marie Pavič' (syn. 'Marie Pavie')

► **Marie Pavič:** Pink in bud with paler pink-tinged double blooms. Also spelt without the accent or as 'Marie Pavie'.

► **Perle d'Or:** A subtle pale apricot double bloom, opening from pointed Tea-rose-type buds.

► **The Fairy:** This award-winning Polyantha (also with a white and red version) has double pink blooms in profusion over healthy foliage.

► **White Pet:** Also known as *R.* 'Little White Pet', this has sprays of double white blooms that open from reddish pink-tinged buds. Glossy foliage.

R. 'Perle d'Or'

R. 'The Fairy'

R. 'White Pet'

Did You Know?

Rosa 'La France', the pink rose discovered in France in 1867 by rosarian Jean-Baptiste André Guillot, is thought to be the first Hybrid Tea and therefore the first of the Modern roses.

Bush Roses

These are the roses that fill our parks, gardens and patios with colour from summer into autumn, producing flower after flower. They include the Hybrid Tea, Floribunda, Patio and modern Miniature roses. The larger-growing Floribundas and Hybrid Teas are typically hard pruned in late winter, as they bloom on the current season's wood.

Hybrid Tea

R. 'Deep Secret'

Once one of the most popular of the Modern roses, a favourite in parks and suburban gardens worldwide, Hybrid Teas gained a bad reputation for disease susceptibility and lack of hardiness. But modern breeding has given gardeners numerous trouble-free cultivars. These roses come in most colours and bicolours and the large, sculpted blooms held singly on long stems are ideal for cutting.

▶ **Deep Secret:** Dark in every way, this upright bush has fragrant fully double and shapely crimson blooms as well as healthy deep green foliage.

▶ **Freedom:** A small, spreading bush with a continual display of chrome-yellow double blooms from late spring to autumn. Light fragrance.

R. 'Freedom'

64

R. 'Indian Summer'

R. 'Moody Blue'

▶ **Indian Summer:** Well-scented, this bush rose's flowers are double and apricot-orange.

▶ **Ingrid Bergman:** A bright red double with healthy foliage, this cultivar has a spicy fragrance.

▶ **Mamma Mia!:** A well-scented coral-orange double flowered Hybrid Tea blooming freely through summer into autumn.

▶ **Moody Blue:** A new rose with good disease resistance and double, highly fragrant blooms in an unusual lilac-mauve.

▶ **Nostalgia:** This plant's eye-catching double blooms have cream petals each edged in cherry red especially towards the outer rings. Healthy and fragrant.

R. 'Mamma Mia!'

R. 'Nostalgia'

Did You Know?

One of the oldest fossil traces of a rose was found in Colorado's appropriately named Florissant Fossil Beds, dated to at least 35 million years ago.

R. 'Papa Meilland'

▶ **Papa Meilland:** A classic, highly fragrant, deep velvety red.

▶ **Pascali:** This is a medium-sized Hybrid Tea with well-shaped creamy white double blooms that are resistant to rain damage. Healthy foliage.

▶ **Pink Perfection:** Fragrant, rich pink double blooms are freely produced on this compact and healthy bush rose.

R. 'Pascali'

R. 'Pink Perfection'

66

R. 'Remember Me'

R. 'Special Anniversary'

R. 'Sunny Sky'

▶ **Polar Star:** A vigorous and floriferous pure white double with good disease resistance.

▶ **Remember Me:** An unusual deep copper orange, this double-flowered Hybrid Tea has a light fragrance and glossy, dark green foliage.

▶ **Special Anniversary:** This has deep rose pink double blooms with a good fragrance and disease resistance.

▶ **Sunny Sky:** Well-formed honey-yellow buds open to paler yellow over healthy foliage.

Did You Know?

The Hybrid Tea rose cultivar *Rosa* 'Double Delight' (syn. 'Andeli'), a red and white bicolour, varies in the shading depending on the amount of sunlight, so you may not end up with a bloom that looks quite like the one on the label!

R. 'Double Delight'

67

R. 'Eyes for You'

R. 'Iceberg'

R. 'Remembrance'

Floribunda

A cross between the Hybrid Tea and Polyantha roses, these carry large clusters of blossoms, some with the classic Hybrid Tea shape, and come in a very wide range of colours. Still a favourite for bedding in parks, modern Floribundas are also extremely popular garden shrubs for mixed-border planting because of their remarkable flower power. More compact Patio roses are often Floribunda types, suitable for containers and small beds.

▶ **Eyes for You:** Semi-double pale lilac with a dark eye and strong perfume.

▶ **Iceberg:** An outstanding pure white semi-double, pink in bud, this rose continues blooming well into autumn. May develop black spot in bad years. Almost thornless. Light scent.

▶ **Remembrance:** This bright red double with a light scent produces copious blooms all season and even tolerates poorer soils.

▶ **Sheila's Perfume:** Growing to 1.2 m (4 ft), this sturdy rose carries Hybrid-Tea-shaped blooms with creamy yellow, red-edged petals that fade to pink. Healthy, with a rich fragrance.

R. 'Sheila's Perfume'

68

▶ **Tickled Pink:** The double blooms are a warm rose pink and have a light scent. Healthy dark green foliage and upright habit to 1.2 m (4 ft).

▶ **Trumpeter:** Compact plants bear clusters of vermilion red blooms in long succession with dark healthy foliage making an excellent foil.

▶ **Valentine Heart:** With light pink-shaded-lilac, wavy-edged petals, this healthy semi-double is a sumptuous garden rose and is fragrant too!

See also page 97–98 for Floribunda roses that go well in mixed borders.

R. 'Tickled Pink'

R. 'Trumpeter'

Miniature

Miniature roses are having something of a renaissance with gardens becoming smaller, and are no longer viewed principally as short-lived houseplants. Normally growing to around 30–45 cm (12–18 in) tall, they flower in flushes through summer and are typically disease-free and hardy. Flower form varies from petite, Hybrid Tea lookalikes to single roses opening flat or semi-double blooms in clusters. Colours range through white, pinks, yellows, reds, oranges and purples, with some two-tone or with a contrasting eye.

Did You Know?

The Grandiflora class of roses popular in the mid-twentieth century included crosses between Hybrid Tea and Floribunda types. Few are commercially available today, but *Rosa* 'The Queen Elizabeth', a tall bush rose, remains popular and typical of the group. Its pink, Hybrid Tea blooms are produced in clusters on long stems – good for cutting, and repeats well.

69

R. 'Cinderella'

R. 'Orange Sunblaze'

R. 'Peter Pan'

- ▶ **Baby Masquerade:** Pale yellow with pink edge, disease-resistant
- ▶ **Cinderella:** Light pink double, fragrant
- ▶ **Diamond Anniversary:** Mauve-pink Hybrid Tea form, light fragrance
- ▶ **Diamond Eyes:** Semi-double dark purple with a white eye, strong fragrance
- ▶ **Little Flirt:** Semi-double red with golden stamens
- ▶ **Medley Ruby:** Red, generously petalled, semi-double
- ▶ **Orange Sunblaze:** Double orange-red, good disease resistance
- ▶ **Violet Cloud:** Single, violet-pink

Patio Roses

This group includes some of the taller Miniature-style rose types as well as short Floribunda and Hybrid Teas typically under 60 cm (2 ft). Examples include the semi-double dark-red-flowered *Rosa* 'Peter Pan' and vivid orange *R.* 'Sunseeker'. For more examples showing the wide range of colours, *see* page 96–97.

R. 'Diamond Eyes'

R. 'Violet Cloud'

Contemporary Climbers and Ramblers

Gardeners today have a wealth of climbing roses to choose from, ranging from the dainty Climbing Miniatures and Patio Climbers to the rampant Ramblers capable of growing up over the roof of a two-storey building. There are many repeat-blooming options, whether you prefer old-rose-style flowers or the simple charm of ruffled semi-doubles or single blooms. Colours are also terrifically varied and fragrance is making a welcome return. Another development is improved flower coverage.

Modern Climbers

The diverse Modern Climbers category includes shrubs, whose long, rather stiff stems can be trained on to horizontal wires or up over frames and structures. They typically produce flowers from the current season's growth and are either cluster-flowered (Floribunda) types or single-bloomed (Hybrid Teas). The latter includes showy specimens such as *Rosa* 'Breath of Life', an apricot-pink fragrant double. The blooms tend to be larger than in old rose climbers and with more reliable repeating. *See* pages 103–04 for more examples.

R. 'Breath of Life'

71

Miniature and Patio Climbers

Though plants from this group of diminutive climbers have been around since the 1950s, there has been a lot of breeding recently, creating small-flowered, dainty-leaved climbers and even some Ramblers for smaller plots and patios. The newer plants have good disease resistance, repeat well and some are also perfumed. In addition, there are several small climbers that do not exactly fit the category, but whose overall size is perfect for squeezing into small spaces.

R. 'Laura Ford'

R. 'Nice Day'

R. 'Purple Skyliner'

▶ **Laura Ford:** An established amber-yellow Climbing Miniature with semi-double blooms to 2.5 m (8 ft). Dark, glossy and disease-resistant foliage.

▶ **Love Knot:** A deep red, lightly fragrant semi-double with flexible stems to 1.8 m (6 ft).

▶ **Nice Day:** A fully double, fragrant, salmon-pink-flowered Climbing Miniature to 2.1 m (7 ft).

R. 'Love Knot'

▶ **Purple Skyliner:** This is a stunning repeat-flowering Rambler with deep purple, white-eyed blooms like a mini R. 'Veilchenblau'. To 2.5 m (8 ft).

▶ **Star Performer:** The lightly fragrant satin-pink blooms of this semi-double Patio Climber rose are produced from top to bottom over the glossy foliage. To 1.8–2.5 m (6–8 ft) high.

▶ **Summertime:** A hard-working, fragrant Patio Climber rose to around 2.1 m (7 ft) with abundant small double yellow blooms that fade to cream.

▶ **Susie:** Large clusters of fully double amber-gold blooms flushed with pink are produced over a long period, with a strong citrus fragrance. To 1.8 m (6 ft).

R. 'Star Performer'

▶ **Warm Welcome:** Semi-double bright orange blooms are produced continuously on this 2.5-m (8-ft) Climbing Miniature, creating an eye-catching feature.

▶ **White Star:** Climbing to 1.8–2.5 m (6–8 ft), this pure white, fragrant semi-double with wavy petals opens to reveal a boss of golden stamens. Happy with any aspect and suitable for a large pot.

Ramblers

R. 'Summertime'

These vigorous roses flowering on the long flexible stems or 'canes' produced in the previous year bloom for just a few weeks in early or mid-summer. A few do repeat. But the volume of the small blooms creates a breath-taking sight and several are wonderfully fragrant. These accommodating roses tolerate shade but need solid support, for example a large tree, substantial pergola or wall with training wires. Colours tend to be muted, but a few, such as the hot pink, white-eyed *Rosa* 'American Pillar', have punch. *See also* 'Ramblers and Their Relatives' on page 105–06.

R. 'American Pillar'

Modern Shrub Roses

Included in this group are veterans whose easy-care attributes make them especially popular today. Many have minimal pruning requirements. Most of the English roses make ideal mixed border plants, but shrub roses can also be used as ground cover in hard-to-manage areas. Some make large specimens with upright or cascading branches, whilst others are short and compact, perfect for smaller plots or for low hedges. Some flower forms and shadings hark back to old roses, whilst others have a wild rose character.

English Roses

Bred by British rosarian David Austin, this immensely popular group of flowering shrubs was created to mirror the opulent flower forms and fragrance of the romantic old roses but to have the positive attributes of Modern roses. They are repeat-blooming, typically with fully double and often quartered blooms, and many have improved disease resistance. Climbing English roses such as the original double pink, *Rosa* 'Constance Spry', have added to the repertoire.

R. 'Abraham Darby'

▶ **Abraham Darby:** Large, fully double-cupped blooms in apricot-shaded pink and yellow with a fruity fragrance are produced over much of the season.

R. 'Graham Thomas'

R. 'James Galway'

▶ **Charles Darwin:** A broad, spreading shrub with fully double quartered blooms of yellow-tinged deeper gold and contrasting dark yellow buds. Tea and citrus perfume.

▶ **Graham Thomas:** Amber-yellow double blooms open from darker pointed buds produced in loose upright clusters. A popular cultivar for cottage and informal country gardens.

▶ **James Galway:** This pale pink quartered double with darker centres makes a short climber or wall shrub or, given light support, an arching shrub perfect for the wild romantic garden.

▶ **Molineux:** A fragrant double yellow with amber tints, this compact grower makes a small shrub rose that repeats well and is disease-resistant. Could be used for a low hedge.

▶ **The Alnwick Rose:** Rich pink, fully double blooms appear in flushes through the season and emit a classic old rose perfume.

See also discussion of English roses in 'Where to Grow Roses' on pages 95, 99–100 and 104.

R. 'Charles Darwin'

R. 'Molineux'

R. 'The Alnwick Rose'

75

Other Modern Repeat-flowering Shrubs

A wide range of shrub roses do not neatly fit into a specific category but have huge value as garden plants and for wildlife-friendly spaces. Some combine traits of old roses with newer breeds and most are easy-care, hardy and repeat-blooming. Singles right through to full doubles are represented here. (*See more* on page 99.)

R. 'Dortmund'

▶ **Dortmund:** Although this sizeable, repeat-flowering shrub can be grown as a climber, its arching stems carrying the large, bright red single blooms make a fabulous feature in a large garden. Each fragrant bloom is highlighted with a white eye, and decorative hips extend the season.

R. 'Golden Wings'

▶ **Golden Wings:** This vigorous repeat-flowering shrub grows to around 1.5 m (5 ft) and has a wild rose look about it. The healthy foliage is light green and the single flowers are soft yellow fading to cream. The stamens are contrasting orange.

▶ **Jacqueline du Pré:** This fragrant shrub rose bears open semi-double blooms with wavy-edged petals that are pure white tinged pink from the buds. Long stamens in pink and gold add detail.

▶ **Knock Out®:** This series of roses growing to 90–137 cm (3–4½ ft) are a group of disease-resistant, hardy, repeat-flowering roses with varying flower forms and colours, mainly available in North America.

R. 'Jacqueline du Pré'

R. Knock Out® ('Radrazz' colour)

▶ **Marguerite Hilling:** A pink semi-double flowered shrub rose growing to 2.1 m (7 ft), this repeat-flowerer is ideal for larger gardens and semi-wild areas. Moderately shade-tolerant.

▶ **Sally Holmes:** A hardy disease-resistant shrub with single, lightly scented blooms, white to very pale pink with apricot-tinged buds, it repeats well and grows to 1.5 × 1.5 m (5 x 5 ft).

R. 'Marguerite Hilling'

Did You Know?

Much of the work on rose cold-tolerance has been carried out in Canada. The Canadian Explorer series and Parkland (Morden) series (the latter grown on their own roots) were developed by an Agriculture and Agri-Food Canada (AAFC) research station. Snow-covered, they survive down to -35°C (-31°F), are mostly disease-resistant, flower in summer with some repeats and generally need little pruning. Singles, semi-doubles and doubles are available. Also check out the hardy and easy-care Buck series.

R. 'Champlain' (Explorer Series)

Groundcover Roses

Also known as 'landscape roses', these are repeat-flowering shrubs, some semi-evergreen, that have a low spreading or mound-forming habit, creating dense cover. There are numerous series and within each, a wide variety of colours and flower forms. Groundcover roses are typically hardy, healthy and easy-care in terms of pruning. Some are bred to be drought-tolerant once established and recent

77

breeding has focused on roses that cope with heat and humidity. (*See* page 112 for more examples.)

R. 'Grouse'

R. 'Rosy Cushion'

R. 'Swany'

▶ **Avon:** One of the County series, this has white, semi-double blooms and pretty pink buds. The foliage is dainty and deep green.

▶ **Grouse:** This landscape rose, a member of the Game Bird series, has glossy deep green foliage and is capable of spreading to 2.5 m (8 ft). The single fragrant blooms are palest pink.

▶ **Pink Flower Carpet:** This semi-evergreen has trusses of semi-double vibrant pink blooms over a long period. Flower Carpet series.

▶ **Rosy Cushion:** Eye-catching single blooms of white edged with vivid pink smother the shrub. Grows to 90 × 120 cm (3 × 4 ft).

▶ **Swany:** A double white-flowered shrub with abundant, dark foliage. Spreads to 1.5 m (5 ft).

▶ **The Fairy:** A Polyantha rose which produces a mass of small double pink blooms on low mound-forming plants. Flowering begins in late summer and continues into autumn.

R. 'Pink Flower Carpet'

R. 'The Fairy'

78

Checklist

▶ **Rose origins:** The oldest fossil rose was found in the US and is 40 million years old. Roses originated in Central Asia and spread through Europe and across to North America.

▶ **Wild roses:** There are around 350 wild rose species, many having wildlife value. Only seven have been used extensively in breeding garden varieties.

▶ **Old Garden roses:** Bred before 1867, these are characterized by a high petal count and often a strong 'old rose' fragrance. Most flower once, between late spring and summer.

▶ **Ancient history:** Damask, Gallica and Alba roses can be traced back to antiquity, and are trouble-free with a strong fragrance.

▶ **China and Tea:** Chinas arrived in Europe during the late eighteenth and early nineteenth centuries, Tea roses being early hybrids. Both repeat but are somewhat tender. Crossbreeding led to Modern roses.

▶ **Modern bush roses:** These are the Hybrid Teas, Floribundas, Patio, Miniature and groundcover roses.

▶ **Modern shrubs:** These include English roses, looking like Old Garden roses, and other repeat-flowering, easy-care cultivars.

▶ **Climbers and Ramblers:** Modern Climbers repeat and have fewer and larger blooms than ramblers or species climbers. Climbing Miniatures have much smaller blooms and leaves. Ramblers bloom once with a profusion of smaller flowers.

Where
to Grow
Roses

Climate Matters

Roses excel in temperate regions of the world where the climate is relatively mild and not too hot in summer. However, such is the appeal of roses globally that gardeners push the boundaries, choosing resilient local varieties and using a range of techniques to protect and nurture this favourite of many. It really pays to do your homework and find out where best to site new roses, and to consider not only the climate but also the microclimate.

Temperature and Humidity

Roses can be found in gardens subjected to widely differing temperatures. Some shrub roses and climbers, especially with wild rose blood, can survive winter temperatures as low as -40°C (-40°F) given shelter and root protection. Meanwhile in hot, dry climates, some roses tolerate summer temperatures of around 37°C (100°F).

When considering where to grow roses, factors to consider include:

▶ **High humidity:** To avoid problems with disease-prone roses, choose cultivars appropriate for your area. For example, the new Knock Out® roses with high black-spot resistance are popular in humid Florida.

▶ **Afternoon shade:** Along with extra watering, shade from the heat of the day enables roses to be grown in hot climates.

▶ **Heat:** Plants lose water more rapidly in hot weather, requiring extra watering, but if conditions are also humid, take care not to overwater.

▶ **Shelter:** Hedging or the walls of the house can protect roses from the cold caused by wind chill and can prevent the desiccation of soft new shoots.

▶ **High summer temperatures:** Roses can shut down and go dormant in sustained hot spells, preventing flowering and new growth.

▶ **Low summer rainfall:** Provided sufficient water is available at the roots, low rainfall and summer humidity help reduce disease. If you have to routinely water roses, water at the base to keep it off the foliage.

Exploring Local Varieties

In areas considered less than ideal for rose growing – too cold, hot, humid or windy – it is vital to seek out species and cultivars that have proven reliability in your location. It is encouraging to note that there will be types that flower well and survive year to year with just a few extra treatments and techniques (*see* pages 204–09).

Some potentially fun ways to discover what plants might thrive in your garden include:

▶ **Visiting local gardens:** Think about getting to know roses in nearby parks and gardens open to the public, including botanic gardens.

▶ **Joining the gardening club:** Mixing with gardeners from your local gardening club or society is a great way to pick up rose-growing know-how.

▶ **Attending flower shows:** Here, you can often talk directly to growers and nursery owners and see a wide range of roses for comparison. Look out for award-winning roses.

▶ **Following rose research:** Look up species and variety recommendations posted by local university and horticultural institutions on the internet.

Aspect

Aspect in gardening refers to the compass direction that walls, fences and borders face. In the northern hemisphere, the conditions are as follows:

▶ **North facing:** Borders with this aspect only get sun at the very beginning and end of the day, so are naturally cool and suitable for shade-tolerant roses.

► **East facing:** These are the next coolest places for growing roses, as they only get morning sun and are in shade through the afternoon. Many roses thrive here.

► **South facing:** Borders, or for that matter house or boundary walls, with this aspect receive sun most of the day and are the hottest and driest. In hotter regions, summer day temperatures can be extreme, so choose heat-tolerant varieties and flowers that don't fade in strong sun. A southerly aspect is a boon in cold regions.

► **West facing:** Here, borders catch the afternoon and evening sun and are warm and sunny, but not so scorching in high summer as south-facing plots.

Did You Know?

Rose trials of new as well as older varieties are carried out in many countries where roses are popular. The various award winners will have exceptional qualities and can be found listed in books and society journals or on the internet. In Britain, for example, the Royal Horticultural Society (RHS) has the Award of Gardening Merit (AGM) scheme and there is also the Rose of the Year award. In the US, the American Garden Rose Selections gives awards to top-performing easy-care, disease-free roses, and the American Rose Society gives the Award of Excellence (AOE) for outstanding miniature roses.

In the southern hemisphere, north is the hottest, sunniest aspect and so on. You will often see roses recommended for different aspects according to the amount of sun or heat tolerated or required.

Microclimate

Whilst you might live in a particularly cold region prone to hard frosts or perhaps a place battered by cold or salt-laden winds, the conditions for growing roses and other plants may be quite different in your

immediate locale, where you might have a protected or favourable microclimate.

Favourable Factors for Colder Regions

The conditions creating a microclimate more suitable for rose growing in cold regions are diverse. The position of the house relative to the garden and most favourable aspect is key, as well as shelter from the prevailing wind.

▶ **Sun-warmed surfaces:** Having a garden with walls or slopes that catch the sun significantly increases light and warmth.

▶ **City living:** Within the warming sphere of a city or its suburbs, temperatures can rise by several degrees due to heat radiated back out into the atmosphere from sun-warmed walls, roads and paving. Gardens may be frost-free, creating Mediterranean conditions.

▶ **Warming water:** Proximity to a large body of water, lake or sea often creates a milder local climate. Coastal regions rarely experience hard frosts.

▶ **Sheltering hillsides:** Protection afforded by surrounding landforms, such as being on the warm, sunny slopes of a sheltered valley, allows a wider range of roses to be grown in cold regions.

▶ **Living screens:** Protection from prevailing cold winds by a tall established hedge or block of woodland makes for improved growing conditions.

Unfavourable Factors for Colder Regions

Some gardens have challenges that you wouldn't expect from looking at the general weather in the region. Problems include:

▶ **Wind turbulence:** Damage is caused by the surrounding buildings creating vortices. This 'wind tunnel' effect is common in urban areas and can adversely affect soft new shoots and flowers and damage roots due to 'wind rock'.

▶ **Cold aspect:** Conditions may be unfavourable for certain roses, especially when additional shade is created by large neighbouring trees or buildings.

▶ **Increased altitude:** The higher you live, the greater the drop in the overall temperature and the shorter the growing season.

Did You Know?

If parts of your garden are at the bottom of a slope, with buildings or dense hedging trapping the cold air that runs down to the base in winter, this can create what is called a 'frost pocket'. Here, temperatures dip dramatically, causing damaging frosts as well as earlier autumn and later spring frosts.

Soil and Drainage

Roses have deep taproots once established and so can survive on many soil types, provided they don't suffer waterlogging in winter. A good depth of a loamy soil, rich in organic matter, is perfect. But clay soils, improved with large amounts of bulky organic matter, can provide all the moisture and nutrients these 'hungry' plants require.

Alkaline or Acid?

Roses prefer soils that are very slightly acidic. If you tested your soil with an inexpensive pH kit from the garden centre, this would be a pH of around 6.5. Most good garden soils hover around the neutral pH7 mark.

Problems can arise for roses when grown in:

▶ **Alkaline soils:** If your soil pH is markedly higher than neutral (pH7), you may find roses show symptoms of nutrient-deficiency, such as yellowing leaves due to the soil chemistry making certain foodstuffs unavailable to the plant.

▶ **Markedly acid:** On peaty soils and the low pH soils sometimes found in high rainfall areas such as upland areas, you may need to adjust the soil pH to make it more alkaline.

Roses for Poor Soils

Soils that are thin and nutrient-poor often lie over solid rock, which might be alkaline or acidic in nature. You can find these soils anywhere, but they are more common in hilly or mountainous areas. Sandy soils and gravelly soils are very free-draining and nutrient-poor, because rain washes foodstuffs down below the root zone. (*See* pages 167 and 168 for improving poor soils.)

Tough Cookies

You can do a lot to improve your soil, but it is best to concentrate your efforts in key areas and use reliable rose varieties in more challenging spots. The following roses and rose groups perform well in poorer, well-drained soils:

Rosa 'Phyllis Bide' is a tough rambler rose

▶ **Species roses:** That is, wild roses or 'pure' roses of natural origin. Also, roses close to their wild ancestors such as the Scottish roses (bred with *Rosa spinosissima*).

▶ **Rambler roses:** For example, 'Albéric Barbier', pale creamy-yellow, double; 'Phyllis Bide', pale apricot-pink, repeat flowering; and 'Super Excelsa', light crimson pink semi-double, repeat flowering.

▶ **Gallica roses:** For example, 'Charles de Mills', crimson-purple, fully double, fragrant; and 'Tuscany Superb', deep magenta-red, semi-double.

▶ **Alba roses:** For example, 'Königin von Dänemark' ('Queen of Denmark'), mid-pink, fully double.

▶ **Hybrid musks:** For example, 'Buff Beauty', amber-yellow to apricot, double.

▶ **Flower Carpet roses:** Groundcover roses, range of colours.

▶ **Knock Out® roses:** Range of colours, doubles and singles.

▶ **The Fairy:** A Polyantha rose, small double blooms, pink.

▶ **Bonica:** A Modern Shrub rose, mid-pink, semi-double with red hips.

▶ **Rugosa roses:** See below.

R. 'Bonica' is another tough cookie

Coastal Rose Growing

Soils on the coast are typically sandy and free-draining and garden plants here may also need to tolerate salt-laden winds. One group of roses thriving in these conditions, provided the soil isn't alkaline, is bred from the naturally healthy Japanese species, *Rosa rugosa*. This has single, fuchsia pink blooms followed by large tomato-red spherical hips. Some fragrant forms and cultivars include:

▶ **Alba:** Single white, hips
▶ **Fru Dagmar Hastrup:** Mid-pink, single, hips
▶ **Blanche Double de Coubert:** White, double
▶ **Sarah van Fleet:** Mid-pink, semi-double, strong fragrance
▶ **Roseraie de l'Haÿ:** Magenta purple, double, strong fragrance

Roses on Heavy Clay

Clay soils are generally poorly drained in winter unless they have been improved and are likely to bake solid in high summer, sometimes cracking as the clay shrinks. One trick for improving drainage on really wet soils is to plant on mounds, raising the roots above the water table. Happily, most roses will cope admirably on heavy clay once drainage has been attended to.

> ## Top Tip
> The soil next to walls is often mixed with rubble and old mortar, and this can increase the dryness and also the soil pH. In addition, the footings of walls may jut out quite a distance from the base, reducing available soil depth. So when planning where to plant wall-trained roses, allow sufficient distance from the wall.
> (*See* pages 171–72.)

Around the Garden

Such is the diversity of roses that you can grow them in most situations. Your style may be formal and perhaps centred around period features, or you may have a more carefree approach. Whatever your inclinations, there are roses to suit.

Factors to Consider

You can find roses that are only a few centimetres tall, ones that spread to form a carpet and ones that are bushy or strongly upright. Climbers may rocket up to the rooftops or fit politely around a small archway. When choosing roses for various situations, consider the following:

▶ **Workload:** How much work and maintenance do you want to do in terms of pruning and deadheading? Will you have to spray the rose to control disease or is it resistant and relatively easy to care for in other ways?

▶ **Ground conditions:** Do you have the right kind of soil? Is it sufficiently fertile and moisture retentive or properly drained?

▶ **Light source:** Will the spot you have earmarked get enough hours of sun?

▶ **Fitting in:** Pay particular attention to ultimate size, as severe pruning can affect flowering performance and looks. Is the rose you have selected going to be the right size ultimately to fill the space?

Roses in Containers

It is often thought that roses make unsuitable subjects for containers because of their deep taproots and need for regular feeding and watering. The majority are in fact quite happy in pots, including a surprising number of shrubs and climbers. Grow them on the patio or within a courtyard where the walls concentrate their fragrance.

Potted Essentials

The popularity of growing roses this way is on the rise and that is partly due to the compact-growing and disease-resistant varieties now available. Also, we understand better just what roses need to flourish.

In order to get the best out of your potted roses and to avoid disappointment, take time to give them the conditions they need:

▶ **Light:** Choose a site in good light with at least a few hours of direct sun during the day, but remember that the sunny walls of nearby buildings can reflect a lot of heat, so a little shade can be beneficial in summer to prevent scorching.

▶ **Pot size:** Provide a large and sufficiently deep pot to accommodate the size and vigour of the rose. Glazing on pots can reduce moisture loss.

▶ **Compost:** Ensure adequate drainage, use a good compost mix and incorporate a sustained release fertilizer. (For more details, *see* pages 189 and 190.)

▶ **Watering:** Roses in pots need a steady supply of water and nutrients, so consider an automatic irrigation system if you have a lot to look after. Some systems allow you to add in an appropriate liquid feed.

Standard roses in pots can be nestled in borders for added drama

Flexible Container Growing

Growing roses in containers allows you to be adventurous and creative. You don't have to have exposed soil in your outdoor space. Pots and planters can be worked in anywhere, but take care that suspended surfaces, such as decks and roof terraces, can support the weight of very large containers.

▶ **No borders?** Grow roses where there aren't any beds or borders, for example on a deck, driveway or concrete yard.

▶ **High rise:** Enjoy romantic rose blooms on a balcony or roof terrace high above ground level.

▶ **Instant seclusion:** Form a living screen around an outdoor seating or dining terrace using potted roses, including standards or climbers trained on frames.

93

▶ **Added drama:** Frame a door or gate with a pair of standard roses or add temporary height to a border.

▶ **Easy moves:** Using pot bases on castors makes potted gardens mobile so that you can ring the changes.

▶ **Change of address:** Growing roses in pots ultimately allows you to take your garden with you if you move house.

Roses for Smaller Containers

▶ **Suitable subjects:** Certain compact-growing rose types lend themselves to being grown in pots, planters and window boxes, although hanging baskets are not suitable. (*See* 'Little Gems' on page 96.)

▶ **Pot size:** Miniature and Patio roses as well as dwarf Polyanthas can be grown in deep 30–60 cm (12–24 in) diameter pots or window boxes.

Did You Know?

There are dainty Patio Climbers for pots, like 'Laura Ford' (pale yellow-tinged amber) and the coral orange 'Warm Welcome' (both around 2.5 m/8 ft) with abundant small blooms. Also consider the pale pink, semi-double called 'Little Rambler', which only reaches 2.25 m (7⅓ ft).

Miniature roses suit growing in pots

Top Tip

Avoid the temptation to mix other plants such as annuals in the same pot as roses. They dislike competition for light, food and root space.

▶ **Table-top roses:** You can use little potted miniatures singly as table centres indoors or out.

▶ **Focal points:** A pot or two of flowers on a deck, perhaps next to a sculpture or figurine, can really draw the eye.

▶ **Staging for effect:** Try displaying pots at different heights, down a flight of steps, say, or use them as part of a larger tiered pot grouping mixed with other patio plants.

Elegant English Roses

In recent years, the English roses, with their old-rose looks but modern repeat-flowering performance, have made a name for themselves as superb patio and courtyard container specimens. The bushier, more compact types that don't need support are ideal and really make an impact in large, deep containers.

R. 'Darcey Bussell' fares well in large containers

Here are some examples:

▶ **Blythe Spirit:** Yellow
▶ **Darcey Bussell:** Deep crimson
▶ **Desdemona:** White
▶ **Harlow Carr:** Mid-pink
▶ **Lady Emma Hamilton:** Apricot
▶ **Princess Anne:** Deep pink
▶ **Roald Dahl:** Apricot

Did You Know?

Many English roses are happy to grow in light shade. Try The Pilgrim, a climber with fragrant yellow blooms (reaches 3.75 m/12 ft]).

Roses for Mixed Borders

There is no need to confine roses to beds used solely to showcase one or more varieties. They are positively enhanced by the contrasting shapes and textures of other blooms and foliage forms. Gardeners today have a wealth of repeat-flowering and disease-resistant bush varieties to work into easy-care mixed plantings.

Little Gems

The relatively new group loosely gathered under the name 'Patio Rose' includes bushy forms that are partway between a Miniature and a Floribunda in character. These typically grow just under 60 cm (2 ft) and are perfect for small and narrow borders or the front of deeper beds. Some listed below are a little over 60 cm depending on climate and conditions, but remain compact. For bags of summer colour, try:

▶ **Amber Queen:** Butter yellow, scented
▶ **Bella Rosa:** Yellow with a touch of pink
▶ **Bright Smile:** Yellow
▶ **Carefree Days:** Mid-pink
▶ **Eyes for You:** Lilac pink with maroon centre, citrus scent
▶ **Gentle Touch:** Pale salmon pink
▶ **Lovely Bride:** Blush pink

R. 'Amber Queen'

- ▶ **Our Dreams:** Creamy white
- ▶ **Peter Pan:** Red, semi-double
- ▶ **Regensberg:** Mid-pink with white edge
- ▶ **Ruby Anniversary:** Red
- ▶ **Sweet Dream:** Pale peach
- ▶ **Top Marks:** Orange-red, double, very compact
- ▶ **White Patio:** White
- ▶ **Wildfire:** Orange

Easy Mixers

The deservedly popular Floribunda roses come in a wide palette of colours and, with multiple smaller blooms per stem produced over a long period, they blend easily with other plants. A number also have a good perfume. Although generally more robust than the Hybrid Teas, it is still worth seeking out the newer disease-resistant varieties such as the vigorous and free-flowering 'Champagne Moment' (cream with an amber tint) as well as established classics such as the white-blushed-pink, lemon-scented 'Margaret Merril'. Good disease-resistant varieties include:

- ▶ **Absolutely Fabulous:** Amber-yellow
- ▶ **Arthur Bell:** Yellow, good fragrance

Did You Know?

Diminutive roses sold as potted houseplants and often given as gifts need not be discarded after flowering. Simply wait for the mild weather and plant out in the garden. Here, they will sometimes grow twice as big and many are surprisingly hardy.

97

- **Blue For You:** Open-centred blooms, soft mauve
- **Champagne Moment:** Cream-tinged amber
- **Easy Does It:** Orange-pink
- **Fragrant Delight:** Coppery salmon
- **Golden Beauty:** Light orangey yellow
- **Golden Smiles:** Warm butter yellow
- **Golden Wedding:** Yellow
- **Happy Retirement:** Light pink, double
- **Hot Chocolate:** Russet-red-tinted brown
- **Lilac Wine:** Pale lilac-pink
- **Lucky:** Hot pink, fragrant
- **Margaret Merril:** Blush pink, fragrant
- **Tatton:** Burnt orange-red, red new growth, fruity scent

Did You Know?

When choosing roses, remember that the shade, health and lustre of the foliage as well as the stem colour can really add to the overall display. Many Floribunda roses, for example, have striking red and purple shaded leaves and shoots on new growth that really complements the flowers.

R. 'Peace'

Sculpted Blooms

Hybrid Tea roses have always been sought after as cut flowers and really stand out with their large pointed buds that spiral open. Although traditionally planted in beds of a single variety, many are striking in mixed borders where their somewhat gawky 'legs' can be partially hidden by surrounding planting. Trouble-free varieties include:

- **Elina:** Pale yellow
- **Chandos Beauty:** Pale apricot pink fading to white
- **Peace:** Creamy with shades of yellow and pink
- **Royal William:** Red

The classic spiralling Hybrid Tea form

- **Savoy Hotel:** Light pink
- **Silver Jubilee:** Rich pink and apricot
- **Thinking of You:** Crimson
- **Warm Wishes (syn. Sunset Celebration):** Apricot

Romantic Leanings

R. 'Joie de Vivre' grows to about 60 cm (2 ft) in height and so is ideal for the front row of borders

English roses and some easy-care shrub roses are perfect for country and cottage-style borders as well as any designed with a romantic flair.

- **Old rose charm:** Though the fully double, quartered roses look like historic varieties, they have improved qualities similar to modern Floribunda and Patio roses.

- **Shrubby habit:** Unlike many Old Garden roses, which often end up with bare 'legs', Modern Shrub and English roses tend to be bushier and clothed with foliage further down.

- **Repeat performance:** Flowering in flushes through most of the summer and into autumn, these roses really earn their space.

- **Height range:** With widely varying heights, you can layer roses using taller types, such as 'Sir John Betjeman', towards the back, and at the front, use plants like 'Joie de Vivre'. Climbers on posts and obelisks add mid-border interest.

- **Vintage perfume:** Many, including the widely grown 'Gertrude Jekyll', have the classic 'old rose' fragrance.

Top Tip

If you have room, try growing English roses in groups of three to eventually merge together as one plant, creating even more impact.

R. 'Golden Celebration'

R. 'Winchester Cathedral'

R. 'Rhapsody in Blue'

Here is a selection of English roses:

▶ **Dame Judy Dench:** Apricot-orange

▶ **Emily Brontë:** Light pink-tinged apricot, new in 2018

▶ **Gertrude Jekyll:** Mid-pink

▶ **Golden Celebration:** Yellow

▶ **Lady Salisbury:** Light pink

▶ **Olivia Rose Austin:** Mid-pink, double

▶ **Pat Austin:** Apricot

▶ **Sir John Betjeman:** Deep red

▶ **The Ancient Mariner:** Mid-pink

▶ **Tranquillity:** White

▶ **Winchester Cathedral:** White.

These are repeat-flowering shrub roses:

▶ **Ballerina:** White with pink edges

▶ **Felicia:** Pink, Hybrid Musk

▶ **Fiona:** Red, semi-double

▶ **Joie de Vivre:** Apricot pink

▶ **Bonica:** Mid-pink

▶ **Blanche Double de Coubert:** White Rugosa rose, double

▶ **Rhapsody in Blue:** Deep purple-red fading to mauve.

R. 'Pat Austin'

R. 'Fiona'

Climbing Roses

Climbing roses come in many sizes, some suited to training over a fence or low wall, others having so much vigour they can cover the front of a two-storey building with ease. They may be set to cascade sumptuously over ornamental structures or simply help camouflage a shed.

High-flying Versatility

You can use the more vigorous climbers and Ramblers in many ways. Grow them up or over the following:

▶ **Trellis or treillage** (ornamental lattice) panel screens around or within a patio or courtyard.

▶ **Pergolas** and other large decorative structures, such as gazebos and wirework pavilions.

▶ **Scented bowers** to create a romantic air in a country setting.

▶ **Larger archways**, perhaps framing a view or forming a rose tunnel.

▶ **Walls** of the house or tall boundaries.

▶ **Rope swags** strung between upright supports in a formal setting.

101

▶ **Sheds and buildings** to camouflage or soften.

▶ **Sturdy trees** or established shrubs for early summer colour.

Modern Flower Power

Today's repeat-flowering climbers are relatively disease-free. Roses in the Modern Climbers and Hybrid Tea groups as well as the climbing English roses and miniature climbers will bloom from early summer through till the hard frosts, given good conditions. Typically, these roses grow to between 2.5 m (8 ft) and 4 m (13 ft).

Depending on their height and vigour, some are suited to:

▶ Low walls, balustrades and picket fences.

▶ **Garden fences:** 1.8 m (6 ft) high fences and trellis panels.

▶ Arches, smaller arbour seats and archways.

▶ **Obelisks:** Made from wire, metal or wood set within a border.

▶ **Pillars:** Wooden posts, treillage or brick pillars within a border or lining a pathway.

▶ **Framing doors and windows:** Trained at lower levels on house walls.

Top Tip

As the base of most climbers tends to lose its leaves over time, revealing bare 'legs', it is a good idea to plant an evergreen shrub in the foreground to fill the gap.

Double Delights

The full, many-petalled blooms of the double Modern Climbers create a lot of impact, especially at the height of flowering. Though these rarely set ornamental hips, many compensate with fragrance.

Here are some you might like to try:

- **Compassion:** Double, coppery-pink and peach, strong fragrance
- **Aloha:** Rich pink, strong fragrance
- **Breath of Life:** Orange
- **Chris:** Yellow, large flowers, fragrant, Hybrid Tea type
- **Dancing Queen:** Bright pink, fragrant
- **Dublin Bay:** Red, good obelisk or pillar rose
- **High Flier:** Red, autumn hips
- **Penny Lane:** Blush pink, strong fragrance, Hybrid Tea
- **Pink Perpétué:** Pink, fragrant
- **Swan Lake:** White-tinged-pink

R. 'Aloha' is a is a fragrant climber

Top Tip

Towards the end of the flowering season, stop removing dead flower heads on single-flowered roses and some semi-doubles so that hips can form. Hips can be quite ornamental, especially en masse and will provide food for the birds during the autumn and winter months.

Singles and Semi-doubles

The more open-centred roses, where the stamens are revealed when fully open, are a boon for insects, especially bees. Single and lightly ruffled semi-doubles are ideal for more relaxed country and cottage-style settings.

Good examples are:

- **Altissimo:** Red, open single blooms
- **Bantry Bay:** Pink, semi-double

103

R. 'New Dawn'

▶ **Golden Showers:** Yellow, semi-double

▶ **Handel:** Semi-double, raspberry and white bicolour, fragrant

▶ **Meg:** Single, pale apricot pink tints over yellow with dark stamens, fragrant

▶ **New Dawn:** Pale flesh pink, semi-double, fragrant, vigorous

▶ **Parkdirektor Riggers:** Single, scarlet red, ornamental hips

▶ **Scent from Heaven:** Salmon-orange, Hybrid Tea type, strong fragrance

▶ **Summer Wine:** Semi-double, coral pink, fragrant

English Climbers

These Modern roses have an old-world charm, not only because of their sumptuous flower forms but also because of the fragrance many of them possess. Unlike some old shrub roses, climbing English roses are repeat-flowering and suffer fewer disease problems.

Good ones to try include:

R. 'James Galway'

▶ **Claire Austin:** Double, white, strong fragrance

▶ **James Galway:** Double, pink

▶ **The Generous Gardener:** Pale pink, semi-double, strong fragrance

▶ **The Pilgrim:** Soft yellow, double

▶ **Wollerton Old Hall:** Double, palest apricot, strong fragrance

▶ **A Shropshire Lad:** Light peachy-pink, double, good fragrance

▶ **Teasing Georgia:** Pale yellow, double, strong fragrance

▶ **Tess of the D'Urbervilles:** Double, crimson red, compact

104

Rambler Power

R. 'Malvern Hills'

Ramblers are known for their vigorous, usually healthy growth and magnificent flower display right down to ground level.

▶ **Spectacular flowering:** Though most bloom only once, albeit over several weeks, the display is breath-taking. Some Ramblers do also repeat.

▶ **Rambler related:** Some repeat-flowering climbers with extra vigour are described as having rambler 'blood'.

▶ **Sky's the Limit:** Ramblers and rambler types have the potential to cover large areas, such as the front of a house or a substantial pergola, and can even scramble up into a tree.

Ramblers and Their Relatives

With their festooning nature, these have huge romantic appeal. The following varieties include true Ramblers as well as those with Ramblers in their breeding history:

▶ *Rosa filipes* **'Kiftsgate':** White, single, strong fragrance, very vigorous to 18 m (60 ft)

▶ **Malvern Hills:** Pale yellow, Rambler hybrid, repeats

Top Tip

If thorns and prickles put you off growing climbers, try one of these: the virtually thornless 'Zéphirine Drouhin' (semi-double, deep cerise pink; *see* page 52); 'Blessings' (a Hybrid Tea type, pink-tinged-salmon); or 'Veilchenblau', a Rambler with single flowers of magenta fading to blue. All have excellent fragrance.

▶ **The Lady of the Lake:** Pale pink, semi-double, repeats, compact growing

▶ **Paul's Himalayan Musk:** Pale pink, semi-double, fragrant, vigorous

▶ **Albertine:** Double, salmon to light pink, fragrant

▶ **Veilchenblau:** Single, magenta-purple with white centres fading to bluish purple, almost thornless

▶ **The Garland:** Cream-tinged blush pink, semi-double, fragrant, orange hips

▶ **Bobbie James:** White, semi-double, orange hips, very vigorous

R. 'Paul's Himalayan Musk'

Did You Know?

Some climbers thrive on cooler, lightly shaded walls and fences, keeping their colour and freshness longer protected from the heat and glare of midday sun. Examples include:

▶ **Danse du Feu:** Double, bright brick red, Modern Climber

▶ **Leverkusen:** Double, creamy yellow, fragrant, Modern Climber

▶ **Paul's Lemon Pillar:** Creamy yellow, double, Hybrid Tea type

R. 'Paul's Lemon Pillar'

Period Piece

Many Old Garden roses evoke a sense of history and are often selected when developing gardens around period properties. But Modern roses tend to repeat their flowering more and have fewer disease problems and have been bred with some of the characteristics of their predecessors, so it is possible to get the best of both.

Getting the Look

As well as some reliable Old Garden roses, for that romantic or vintage look, you may want to choose:

► **Contemporary shrub roses:** Select forms with fully or semi-double blooms and abundant healthy foliage.

► **English roses:** *See* pages 95 and 100.

► **Vintage colouring:** The more delicately shaded or deep, velvet-red coloured Floribundas and Hybrid Teas – such as the single, lilac-pink 'Sweet Haze' – fit right in with antique schemes.

► **Climbing simplicity:** Pick wall shrubs and climbing roses with abundant single or semi-double blooms, such as Ramblers and Rambler hybrids.

107

Formal Gardens

In formal settings, it is common to grow roses in clearly defined beds that showcase the roses, with other plants taking a supporting role. Larger ornamental structures, perhaps over main pathways, may support old shrub roses, Ramblers and other types of climbing rose. Add height to beds with compact climbers suitable for pillars and obelisks, or use carefully placed standard roses. (For formal garden designs and features, *see* pages 128–29.) Suitable old shrub roses for beds include:

The Portland shrub rose, *R.* 'Comte de Chambord' works well in formal beds

▶ **Gallica and Damask:** Once-flowering
▶ **Moss:** Once-flowering
▶ **Portland and Bourbon:** Repeat-flowering
▶ **Noisettes and Hybrid Perpetuals:** Repeat-flowering

Herb Gardens

Roses have a long history of being grown in herb gardens, valued for their fragrance as well as their medicinal and culinary properties. Herbs generally enjoy sharply drained (very well drained), even poor soil and sunny conditions. Choose roses of historic significance, ones with a strong fragrance as well as roses that enjoy the same conditions as Mediterranean herbs:

▶ **The apothecary's rose:** *Rosa gallica* var. *officinalis* can be traced back to medieval monasteries. It is a fuchsia pink, 1.2 m (4 ft) high, easy-to-care-for shrub, flowering once over a long period.

▶ **Rosa mundi:** Equally as famous as the apothecary's rose is the white-striped *Rosa gallica* 'Versicolor', commonly known as rosa mundi.

108

▶ **Drought-tolerant roses:** Some of the roses from the 'Tough Cookies' list on page 89 revel in poor conditions.

▶ **Scented old roses:** Consider varieties of English rose such as the pink 'Boscobel' and 'Harlow Carr' and the dark red-purple 'Munstead Wood'.

R. 'Munstead Wood' is a lovely, scented choice for a herb garden

Flowering Hedges

Low hedges smothered in blooms are ideal for separating and screening areas within the garden and for use along boundaries. Rose hedges aren't as neat as other formal garden classics like box, beech, holly and yew, but make up for it with the sheer abundance of blooms. Rose hedges can be kept as low as 0.76 m (2½ ft) to 1.8 m (6 ft), depending on variety and how hard they are trimmed. Try the following English and shrub roses:

▶ **Harlow Carr:** Mid-pink, double, strong fragrance, English

▶ **Queen of Sweden:** Pale pink, double, English

▶ **Wildeve:** Pale pink, double with densely packed petals, English

▶ **The Mayflower:** Mid-pink, double, strong fragrance, English

▶ **Cornelia:** Peachy pink and apricot, semi-double, fragrant, Hybrid Musk

▶ **Hansa:** Magenta pink, highly fragrant double with hips. A long-flowered Rugosa

▶ **Teasing Georgia:** Yellow, fully double, English

▶ **Crocus Rose:** Very pale apricot to cream, double, English

▶ **Sophy's Rose:** Deep pink, double, English

▶ **Scabrosa:** Lilac-pink, single, large colourful hips, Rugosa

▶ **Wilhelm:** Deep crimson double, hips, fragrant, Hybrid Musk

R. 'Harlow Carr' is a suitable choice for a rose 'hedge'

109

Gardening With Nature

Large, gracefully arching shrub roses, groundcover roses and Ramblers make wonderful additions to the wild garden. Meadow gardens can lack colour and fragrance during the summer months. By planting the right roses, you can add visual interest as well as greatly benefiting nature.

Wild Garden Choices

Many of the wild species and their near relatives, as well as Old Garden roses that need minimal care, work well in wild gardens. You can let more vigorous Ramblers scramble up into a tree. Maximize benefits to wildlife by:

▶ **Planting hedging:** When ordering country mix hedging from nurseries to plant in winter, specify a proportion of wild roses.

▶ **Utilizing poor ground:** Plant tough, drought-resistant roses.

Hips from Rosa rubiginosa. Planting roses that produce plentiful hips, such as this wild rose, is good for wildlife

110

▶ **Adding simple blooms:** Select roses with masses of small single or semi-double blooms. Full doubles don't usually benefit pollinators.

▶ **Selecting roses with hips:** Choose shrub roses and climbers like the white Rambler 'Francis E. Lester' or the red-flowered *Rosa* 'Geranium' (*moyesii* hybrid) that produce plentiful hips.

▶ **Creating habitat:** Cover slopes and difficult-to-access areas with low, ground-hugging roses as well as more vigorous types that form large, impenetrable mounds. These areas provide shelter and bird nesting sites.

Groundcover Roses

Groundcover roses are often used for landscaping hard-to-manage areas. They are useful for:

▶ **Garden fringes:** Plant on the margins of the garden, where garden maintenance has become more relaxed and infrequent. Pruning can be done with a hedge-trimmer!

Did You Know?

Single and semi-double blooms provide ample nectar for foraging bees and other insects, and many then go on to produce attractive hips that help feed birds and mammals through autumn and winter

▶ **Driveways:** Use as foreground planting either side of long driveways fringed by trees and shrubs.

▶ **Banks:** Replace sloping and hard-to-mow lawns.

▶ **Rock gardens:** Cascade over large, naturalistic rock and stream gardens.

Star Varieties

Some of today's best groundcover roses have outclassed older varieties like the mid-pink, single 'Max Graf' and pale pink, single 'Nozomi' by prolonging the flowering. Several also have semi-evergreen foliage.

Healthy and reliable varieties include:

▶ **Flower Carpet Amber:** Amber-yellow, semi-double

▶ **Flower Carpet Coral:** Coral pink, single

▶ **Flower Carpet Red Velvet:** Deep scarlet, single, golden stamens

▶ **Flower Carpet White:** Pure white, semi-double

▶ **Flower Carpet Gold:** Golden yellow ruffled blooms, semi-double

▶ **Magic Carpet:** Pink, semi-double

▶ **Kent:** White, semi-double

▶ **Surrey:** Rich pink, semi-double

▶ **Suffolk:** Dark scarlet red, single, hips

▶ **Worcestershire:** Yellow, semi-double

▶ **Partridge:** White, single, hips, vigorous spreader

Did You Know?

Some shrub roses bear attractive red translucent thorns that shine with winter backlighting and look superb in wild garden settings. A prime example is *R. sericea* subsp. *omeiensis* f. *pteracantha*, the winged thorn rose.

Checklist

▶ **Climate considerations:** Some roses tolerate cold and heat, humidity, rainfall and exposure to wind or salt spray. Many Old Garden roses, Modern Shrub roses and Ramblers are tough.

▶ **Local varieties:** Get to know which roses suit your region and look for award-winners or roses bred to suit your specific conditions.

▶ **Aspect and microclimate:** Explore your garden's microclimate to seek out favourable sites. Avoid frost pockets and wind tunnels.

▶ **Soil and drainage:** What is your soil type and pH? Identify trouble spots.

▶ **Containers and patios:** Select compact and free-flowering roses for maximum impact in small spaces.

▶ **Roses in mixed borders:** Pick easy-care varieties with the right habit and flowering potential to blend in.

▶ **Climbers:** Select varieties that grow to the right size for the spot you have earmarked.

▶ **Period charm:** In formal or period gardens, choose Old Garden roses, or Modern roses with vintage character.

▶ **Wild gardening:** Use wild species and single-blooming roses for pollinators, birds and mammals. Large Old Garden roses, Ramblers and shrub roses are less formal.

▶ **Low maintenance:** Plant healthy, long-flowering, drought-tolerant groundcover roses.

Designing With Roses

Achieving Balance and Harmony

Whether you are planning an area that focuses entirely on roses or one that blends roses with a host of other plants, there are a number of factors that will help to bring out the best from both the space and the roses. Roses can be the main event or supporting cast but, either way, how they are presented has a major impact on the overall success of a garden.

Garden Footprint

It is critical to get a garden's 'footprint' (layout) right when designing a new area – it is much easier than adapting at a later date. Do some research on the various style options and, when you are ready to start working on the layout, consider the following:

▶ **Scale and proportion:** Designs should be functional with room in borders for the roses and other plants to spread out comfortably. Try to achieve a balance between the open, non-planted spaces, such as lawns, pools and patios, and the borders and hedges.

▶ **Pathways:** Remember that foreground and edging plants tend to sprawl over pathways, so take this into account when setting out.

Low bordering hedges such as box also 'creep' with age, gradually overhanging paths. The paths may look too wide at first, but will soon feel to scale.

▶ **Access for maintenance:** Ensure you can get behind planting for hedge trimming, for training roses and other climbers and for window cleaning or wall painting. In deep borders, consider adding a simple hidden central pathway for maintaining the plants either side.

▶ **Divisions:** Larger spaces and long narrow gardens can be broken up to create a series of garden 'rooms', each with comfortable proportions and perhaps planted and dressed to reveal a different mood or character.

Top Tip

Before committing to a design, consider the garden's 'bones'. Imagine what the garden will look like in winter. Is the overall layout and pattern of paths and beds pleasing? Are there sufficient vertical elements, such as formal hedges and trellis screens, to maintain interest?

Green Walls

Especially with gardens devoted to rose growing, it is important to have a simple backdrop or series of dividing walls to provide a foil for the blooms. These traditionally come in the form of clipped formal hedging – yew, box, privet, hornbeam and so on. Low evergreen hedges also help to contain the roses, creating a sense of ordered calm and hiding the bare 'legs' of lanky bush or shrub roses.

Green 'walls', such as yew hedges, provide a foil for the contrasting blooms of roses

117

Planning Garden Structures

Rose gardens typically employ at least one type of structure or framework over which climbers and lax shrub roses can be trained. In small plots, this might be something like an archway or some trellis obelisks. Larger structures include pergolas, wirework rose pavilions and gazebos or arched tunnels to flow roses over a pathway.

Before purchase or construction, consider the following:

▶ **Trial run:** Ornamental structures can be expensive, so work out if they are the right size and scale. Use long bamboo canes and twine to mock up an approximate copy in the same position. View the mock-up from different angles and live with it for a few days before buying the real thing.

▶ **Head height:** With pergolas and other overhead structures, imagine the room-like quality they give to the space. Is there sufficient head height to the 'ceiling' to avoid the space feeling claustrophobic? Around 2.4 m (8 ft) is a good starting point. Remember that stems will trail down below the struts, reducing head height.

▶ **Trellis screens:** Trellis panels can divide up the space and create privacy between one area and another, but they still let light through and provide a ready-made framework on which to train roses and other climbers.

▶ **Making an entrance:** Single arches and gateways always look better positioned if they are physically connected to existing hedges, walls or other garden dividers.

118

Materials Palette

The range of materials used in construction
has a major influence on the look of the
garden. Keep things simple by limiting the
elements selected. Your choices should tie
in comfortably with the main building and its
outbuildings and even with local or vernacular
architecture. However, don't be afraid to
dovetail a contemporary garden design with
an older property.

Focal Points

Use key features to draw the eye
through the garden. For example, at
the end of a rose 'tunnel' walkway,
place a bench seat, a large pot or a
piece of sculpture. Other decorative
elements can be used to signal a
transition from one area to another,
perhaps involving a change in level.
Path intersections present numerous
opportunities for eye-catching focal
points. In formal gardens, you could try
a wirework gazebo or cobble mosaic.

Secret Garden

Create a sense of mystery and make the space feel larger by introducing areas that aren't immediately visible from the main path or viewpoint. This is particularly useful with long narrow gardens, where the eye tends to race to the end unless slowed by visual trickery.

► **Bays in deep borders:** By pushing a rectangular or semi-circular section of border back from the path towards the boundary, you can create secret spaces, partially hidden by the surrounding planting. In a small 'insert', you could accommodate an ornamental birdbath, say. Or in a larger 'pocket', a bench or bistro table and chairs.

► **Curving pathways:** Let a footpath lead the eye round into a hidden corner, encouraging the urge to explore. Don't disappoint though. Make sure the journey is rewarded with a surprise element! Alternatively, meander a pathway or central lawn all the way down the garden, creating a series of spaces partially obscured by deeper sections of border and taller blocks of planting.

► **Dividing walls:** Form discrete spaces within the plot using trellis screens and hedges punctuated with arches, gates and doorways. These allow tantalizing glimpsed views into other areas. You can even train or clip 'windows' through hedges.

Working With Colour

Colour is of prime importance in design. It influences our emotional state, helping to create a certain atmosphere or feel within the garden. Roses are mostly in shades found at the warm end of the spectrum – reds, oranges, yellows and clear or salmon pinks. The cooler lilacs, mauves and purple-reds carry hints of the elusive blue. There are relatively few pure white roses; most are white or cream tinted with pink, yellow or peach, the colour more pronounced in bud.

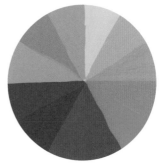

Top Tip

You may only need a few splashes of a complementary colour to bring a tightly colour-schemed border alive. These 'pops' of colour may be provided by objects other than plants, such as a ceramic pot, painted obelisks or a bench seat.

Using the Artist's Colour Wheel

If you take a colour on the artist's wheel, such as scarlet red, looking either side of that colour provides you with shades that blend well together. On the opposite side to red is green. Green is the complementary colour for red and provides the greatest contrast and drama when combined in the border.

Other complementary pairs are:

▶ Soft lilac and pale yellow or cream

▶ Orange with clear bright blues and turquoise

▶ Golden yellow with rich purple.

121

Painting With Roses

It is rewarding to experiment with particular colours of roses in combination with other plants. You can create different atmospheres within a garden, or enliven a plant grouping with just a few added tints.

Here are some of the mood-enhancing effects you can create:

▶ **Pastels:** Groups of roses in pastel shades work well together and have a calming effect.

▶ **Dark highlights:** A few deep velvet red roses lift plantings of mainly pale pastel blooms.

▶ **Cool elegance:** White and cream roses create an elegant, cooling atmosphere within a restricted palette of greens and silvers, with dark purple or maroon-red foliage highlights.

▶ **Modern mix:** Bright yellow roses associate well with stronger 'hot' pinks, violet, delphinium blues and touches of orange for a lively, contemporary vibe.

Roses can provide rich hits of dark, mysterious colour

Top Tip

If you use eye-catching white or 'hot' coloured roses like orange, scarlet and golden yellow, it is best to position them closer to the house rather than at the end of the plot, otherwise they can foreshorten the view. Using softer, blue-tinted shades such as deep crimson or lilac towards the boundary makes the space feel longer.

▶ **Tropical heat:** Clear orange and scarlet-red roses mix with bold red-, purple- and maroon-flushed architectural foliage plants for a sub-tropical twist.

▶ **Reflective mood:** Dark crimson, blood red and purple-tinted roses combined with foliage plants suffused with bronze, plum and red helps to create a sense of mystery.

These pastel roses make for a pleasing contrast with the burnt umber of the painted brick

Coloured Backdrops

Building materials and finishes used on the house exterior, garden walls, timber structures and outbuildings may be strongly coloured – painted render, for example. Take these backdrops into account when selecting the shade of a climbing rose or elements in a mixed border.

Top Tip

White and cream roses, pale yellow and pale pastel coloured roses are more visible than other shades at twilight. Something to consider if your garden is mainly used in the evenings.

123

Around the Home

It is very appealing to introduce the sight and scent of roses to the home. The zone around the front door is key. Here, roses could be trained beneath windows or around a porch or veranda. A pair of potted rose standards is formal but welcoming at the front of a town house. In the more private back gardens and secluded courtyards, yet more possibilities unfold.

Front of House

Roses mostly need good soil and plentiful moisture to thrive and these conditions aren't always available right next to the front door, or under the windows, especially with competition for space from parking and access.

Improve your displays by giving roses the following:

▶ **A good start:** Make beds right next to the house wall as deep as possible, so that the dry 'rain shadow' area can be avoided. Dig out any rubble and add bulky organic matter to retain moisture.

▶ **Room to grow:** Take care when positioning new roses, especially more vigorous varieties. You don't want to be fighting your way through thorny branches in a year or two or blocking light through windows.

▶ **Firm support:** Put up a sturdy framework of wires and vine eyes (screws or nails with a loop on the end to which to attach wires) or erect trellis panels (*see* pages 101–02). Ensure that arches and other structures are strong enough to support the fully grown plant.

▶ **Kerb appeal:** Consider a richly perfumed rose-covered arch over the entrance gate or path to welcome visitors. Where gardens are more open and informal, how about a rose hedge next to the pavement?

Watching the World Go By

A seat on a porch or covered veranda can provide the perfect vantage point from which to survey and admire your front garden and even chat to passers-by if the house is visible from the street. Add to the relaxed ambience with beautiful displays of fragrant roses.

Raised Vantage Point

Looking down from a porch or veranda on to beds of roses

125

and other plants enables you to study the blooms in more detail. Symmetrical beds either side of steps to the front door can be planted with just one variety for impact.

A Little Privacy

Taller shrub and bush roses could help with screening and you can also fill in gaps between a veranda's floor, or handrail, and roof with lattice panels supporting climbing roses.

Courtyards

Although space may be limited, a courtyard garden affords privacy and can have a very calm atmosphere away from the hubbub of urban living. Keep your design simple, perhaps with raised beds around the walls to allow for planting if the floor is solid. The sight and sound of a rill or small fountain add to the relaxed ambience.

Here are some tips for courtyard growing:

▶ **Large pots:** Especially if you don't have borders, plant up single large pots or a small pot grouping, planting each container with a repeat-flowering shrub rose (*see* page 74–77) or compact climber.

▶ **Overhead training:** Create a room-like feel without cutting out too much light by running tensioned wire cables between the walls at ceiling height and training climbers, including roses, up the walls and overhead.

▶ **Raised beds:** Patio roses (*see* page 96) as well as English and other shrub roses recommended for containers (*see* pages 94–95) are ideal for raised beds, as their growth is compact with good foliage cover. These and the new breeds of groundcover roses flower right through summer into autumn.

Did You Know?

Moist air captures and concentrates fragrance, which is why moving-water features and fountains are often added to rose gardens and flower-filled courtyards.

Indoor-Outdoor Living

Patios and terraces represent the transition zone between the house and garden. Their style and the choice of materials usually reflects the house, and all-weather hard surfaces predominate for reasons of practicality and aesthetics. At the same time, the garden is drawn in closer through the use of patio pots and planters, raised beds and climber-covered pergolas. Whether sunny or shaded for part of the day, this zone can be filled with fragrant flowers, including many different types of rose from Miniature to Rambler.

127

Garden Styles

How you lay out, plant and furnish your garden is very much a matter of personal taste, though the location and architecture of the house and the form of the surrounding landscape will usually have a bearing. Roses are often associated with formal and period designs as well as country garden aesthetics, but there is no reason you can't enjoy roses in a contemporary or urban setting.

Simply Formal

A strong geometric footprint, with pathways acting as sight lines to focal points, characterizes formal gardens, whether period in style or contemporary. The walled garden theme is alluded to by tall clipped hedging and low barriers, typically of box or yew, to contain the roses. Garden architecture and symmetry prevail. Other formal features might include:

▶ **A rosarium or roseraie:** These are gardens devoted to growing roses and typically have one rose type in each bed or box-edged compartment.

▶ **Ornamental structures:** Often gazebos and pavilions are manufactured from metal, allowing for complex decorative touches and paint finishes. You might also consider arched tunnels for a fragrant rose walkway or a timber pergola decorated with finials and treillage.

▶ **Pools and fountains:** Water is an essential element in a formal garden, whether it is something simple like a shallow, reflecting pool or a lively fountain.

▶ **Topiary:** Evergreen plants, such as boxwood, yew, holly and, in warmer climes, *Phillyrea* (false olive), myrtle and bay, are clipped into traditional geometric shapes such as balls and domes, obelisks, cones and cake stands. Formal clipped hedging is also a form of topiary.

▶ **Formal lawns:** Usually these are bowling-green-perfect, geometrically shaped and act as a foil for the varicoloured roses in the surrounding beds.

▶ **Rhythmic elements:** Establish a visual rhythm using pillars and columns of brick, stone or treillage set equidistantly, in a straight line, arc or circle. Link pillars and posts with rope swags to carry climbers and Ramblers.

A Little Bit Country

It is possible to select elements of the country house or cottage garden even if you live in the city. Perhaps a rose-covered pergola with a stone-flag pathway? Or if you hanker for a cottage garden, why not start with roses round the door?

Country House Elegance

With a little theatrical camouflage, you can work with your house façade and conjure that look of faded elegance. Much of the garden architecture is similar to that of formal gardens but rather less rigid and manicured.

▶ **Framework planting:** If there is space, split the plot into garden 'rooms' enclosed by walls of hedging, punctuated by archways and connected by walkways, tunnels and rose-covered pergolas. Traditionally beech, hornbeam, lime, holly and yew were used, but there are alternatives for warmer climates.

▶ **Lawns:** Use mown grass to connect hard surfaces with borders. Lawns may incorporate changes in level rather than being terraced, though a flight of stone steps could provide a focal point. Lawn daisies add to the relaxed ambiance.

▶ **Wild touches:** Areas of long grass, naturalized spring bulbs and wild flowers are common in orchards or on the garden boundaries, but keep the line between mown lawn and long grass defined. Allow ferns and other wild plants to colonize cracks in steps and walls, softening hard lines.

▶ **Vintage rose appeal:** Country gardens are the perfect setting for billowing romantic roses such as the Hybrid Musks, double-flowered Ramblers and full-petalled English roses, as well as many other Modern Shrub roses. And don't forget rose hedges.

▶ **Materials and colour palette:** Look for worn or weathered-look paving and walling materials, including large planters for roses which could be in faux lead. Select structures and furniture in metal or timber in muted shades – French grey, for example – for a vintage feel.

Cottage Gardens

True cottage gardens, unlike the chocolate box fantasies, were simply designed plots with narrow access paths forming a grid pattern and very little wasted space. These gardens were about practicality and making do. Cottage-inspired gardens have a number of common themes:

▶ **Topiary:** A nod to the Lord of the Manor's house, gardeners of old would shape wild hedgerow plants into forms like chickens and pheasants.

▶ **Boundary issues:** Hedges were often multi-purpose, protecting the property and containing animals as well as providing foodstuffs and medicines. Painted picket fences as well as simple barriers of woven hazel hurdles offer a space-saving alternative and support for lax roses.

▶ **Planting mix:** Cottage gardens traditionally had a mix of wild and cultivated plants, fruit, vegetables and herbs. Plants for making household products and toiletries as well as medicines were grown, and sweet-smelling wild roses and honeysuckle masked unpleasant smells!

▶ **Repurposed materials:** Follow in the old cottage gardener's footsteps by using reclaimed bricks for pathways, old timbers for rustic seating, and containers that once had another use as planters for old-fashioned looking roses – a washing dolly tub, for example.

Wild Romance

In a spacious wild garden, perhaps on the fringes of a more ordered plot or in a disused orchard, shrub roses and rambunctious climbers can sprawl and luxuriate. You may just spot the remnants of human activity, such as an old metal farm gate or dilapidated bench seat through a mist of grasses and wild flowers.

▶ **Borrowed landscape:** By camouflaging the true boundary of the garden, covering simple wire fencing or drystone walls with exuberant semi-wild roses and other hedgerow plants, you can increase the size of your plot by incorporating elements of the landscape beyond.

► **Rustic touches:** Structures such as a rose bower or pergola walkway, as well as furniture pieces, blend in better when made from natural materials or when rusted or distressed. Use heavy, rough-sawn or live-edge timbers and rustic poles. Weave rose supports from hazel and willow.

► **Mown pathways:** Access tends to be informal, but you can maintain a sense of order by mowing a network of paths through the long grass.

Modern Directions

Today's trend is to connect with the garden. Level access on to decks and terraces and retractable large glass doors blur the threshold. You might still see formal hedges, even simple geometric topiary, but the planted infill is likely to be soft textured and inspired by wild landscapes. Some modern garden elements include:

► **Simple planting:** Roses and their companions are selected from a limited palette of plants set in larger groups of fives, sevens, nines and so on.

► **Natural look:** Roses may be surrounded by a matrix planting of ornamental grasses mixed with wild-looking perennials, giving a softer, more meadow-like feel

► **Outdoor living:** Integrated seating, perhaps around a sunken fire pit, ensures that people use the garden like another room when the weather permits. Subtle lighting enables night-time use.

► **Inspired construction:** Materials for hard landscaping may be reclaimed, have a distressed industrial finish or vintage look, but will be laid in contemporary, often rectilinear patterns and mixed with modern elements like glass.

Checklist

▶ **First steps:** Design the garden's footprint, its paths, lawns, borders and so on with pleasing proportions and practicality in mind. Mock up proposed structures.

▶ **Garden rooms:** Plant hedges as a backdrop for roses and use them along with walls and trellises to create separate spaces.

▶ **Choosing materials:** Keep the palette simple, reflecting the house or local architecture.

▶ **Colour wheel:** Find the right colours to tone or contrast with roses and create a scheme.

▶ **Around the house:** Welcome visitors with fragrant roses in pots or trained round doors, or plant in beds beside terraces and pathways.

▶ **Formal styles:** Use a simple geometric template. Low hedges define the beds. Add a strong focal point.

▶ **Country house or cottage:** Develop a simple, semi-formal plan with hedges and topiary, but plant in a romantic style. For cottage style, keep to a no-frills layout and use rustic or reclaimed materials. Mix edibles, herbs and perennials with roses.

▶ **Wild and romantic:** Camouflage garden boundaries and, where possible, incorporate a view of surrounding countryside. Plant shrub roses and Ramblers within long grass.

▶ **Modern:** Keep hard landscaping simple. Use reclaimed or industrial finishes; bold blocks or go naturalistic.

Rose
Companions

A Modern Approach

Not so long ago in the history of rose growing, the idea of mixing roses with other plants was almost unheard of. Rose beds would be edged with box and lavender hedging or other knot garden herbs, but the ground beneath and between was largely kept bare. Roses were to be admired and given pride of place in their own beds. Today, roses are valued for their partnerships with a host of different flowers.

In the Mix

Growing roses with other types of shrubs and climbers considerably increases the season of interest and makes for creative colour scheming. What is more, with so many perennials, biennials and bulbs to choose from, as well as annuals and patio plants, your growing options are endlessly varied. When planning what to grow alongside your roses, consider the following:

▶ **Similar likes and dislikes:** Check that plants have the same broad requirements for soil type and moisture, light levels, heat tolerance and hardiness. In the US, compare hardiness zones.

▶ **Flowering time:** It seems obvious, but if you are designing schemes reliant on various colours and forms coinciding for effect, you need to be sure the flowering times generously overlap.

▶ **Form and texture:** The supporting cast for showier roses shouldn't compete, rather their differing habit, foliage and flower forms should subtly support and enhance the blooms.

136

▶ **Colour:** You might not be consciously employing a colour scheme, but certain shades do work better with others (*see* page 121). Good combinations really lift a border or patio arrangement.

Contrasting Habit

Although some bush and shrub roses are quite upright with sparse foliage, many more have a mounded habit, densely clothed with leaves, and generally look more horizontal and spreading than vertical. More rounded forms of roses contrast well with uprights, such as:

▶ **Columnar evergreens:** Conifers such as fastigiate yews (*Taxus baccata* 'Fastigiata') or Italian cypress (*Cupressus sempervirens* Stricta Group) give a Mediterranean or formal look.

▶ **Tall perennials:** In many taller perennials, such as delphiniums and verbascum, as well as biennials, such as hollyhocks and foxgloves, you will see the trend is strongly upright. Some bulbs and corms also provide vertical accent – lilies, gladioli and *Crocosmia* 'Lucifer', for example .

▶ **Roses on pillars and obelisks:** Vertical structures softened by climbing roses add height to mixed borders without taking up a lot of space.

▶ **Summer bulbs:** Whether left in the ground over winter or replaced/replanted annually, many of the taller summer- and autumn-flowering bulbs have an upright habit.

▶ **Ornamental grasses:** With their narrow linear foliage and tall airy flower heads, grasses are increasingly popular partners for roses, especially in contemporary settings.

Tall perennials such as delphiniums contrast well with shorter roses

137

Flower Forms

Roses are extremely varied in form, from the almost flat circles of single blooms, to the bowl-shaped semi-doubles with a central 'boss' of stamens. Doubles range from the dense pom-poms of some Old Garden roses and their lookalikes to the spiralling Hybrid Tea form. Blooms may be small and numerous, in clusters or held singly. All this needs to be considered when finding suitable perennial matches.

Bloom Contrasts

Generous multi-petalled rose heads are quite solid, so look well with airy flowers. Alternatively, pick a different shape such as the flat plates of achillea, daisies or salvia spires. Team the multiple smaller blooms of various climbing, shrub and bush roses with larger, sculptural blooms like bearded iris or peony.

Digitalis (foxglove) with roses

Spires, Wands and Pokers

The narrow, upright flower forms of certain perennials, as well as biennials like the foxglove, work well with roses in general. With their predominantly blue and purple spikes, salvias, delphiniums, aconites and agastache are ideal with rose colours.

▶ **Aconite:** The hooded blooms of monkshood are typically deep purple-blue or white, the latter standing out well in shade. *Aconitum* 'Stainless Steel' is pale blue-grey. Poisonous.

▶ **Agastache:** The fluffy spikes of giant hyssop are bee magnets. With roses grow the moderately hardy blue-purple 'Blackadder' and 'Blue Fortune' (well-drained soil and full sun). Plants self-seed if not deadheaded and may be a problem in warmer climates as garden escapees.

▶ **Delphinium:** These tall blue columns are a mainstay of the cottage-garden border. Compact selections like the Magic Fountains series can be used towards the front of the border. Early to mid-summer flowering. Poisonous.

Kniphofia with roses

▶ *Digitalis* (foxglove): Though the deep pink *Digitalis purpurea* and pure white *D. p.* f. *albiflora* are excellent in the semi-wild garden, for subtle hues with early shrub roses, try the mixed pastels of *D. purpurea* Excelsior Group and the charming *D. p.* 'Sutton's Apricot'. Biennial. Shade-tolerant. Poisonous.

▶ **Kniphofia:** The large, sub-tropical-looking torch lily has been replaced in many gardens by grassy leaved versions with dainty pokers, such as those in the Popsicle series.

▶ **Salvia:** *Salvia nemorosa* 'Caradonna' (deep purple blue) and *S. n.* 'Amethyst' work well with medium-sized shrub and English roses. The shorter 'Mainacht' and 'East Friesland' (both deep purple blue) are perfect sunny border partners for vibrant bush and Patio roses.

▶ *Sidalcea*: Known as prairie mallow, these miniature hollyhock lookalikes are available in white or pinks, for example 'Elsie Heugh' (pale pink) and 'Party Girl' (deep rose pink).

▶ *Sisyrinchium striatum*: The creamy flower spikes and fans of grey-green foliage would make the perfect foreground for lilac roses. *S. s.* 'Aunt May' has cream striped leaves. Requires well-drained soil and full sun.

Sisyrinchium striatum with roses

139

▶ **Verbascum**: Although mainly yellow, mulleins come in buff, pink, mauve or apricot shades. The white nettle-leafed mullein *V. chaixii* 'Album' is a gem. Its mid- to late-summer spires are ideal in the semi-wild or cottage garden, where it can self-seed. Good on dry soils, but avoid acidic.

▶ **Veronicastrum**: Forms of *V. virginicum*, for example 'Pink Glow' and 'Lavendelturm', are statuesque plants that flower mid- to late summer or early autumn. Best given moisture-retentive soil.

Bells and Trumpets

The bellflowers (*Campanula*) are one of the groups traditionally grown with roses in cottage and country house borders. The mainly blue and lilac shades make a pleasing foil. Darker purple penstemons such as 'Blackbird' and 'Raven' work especially well with pastel or deep crimson roses, and bloom for months if deadheaded. For drama, add large-flowered lilies and day lilies.

▶ *Campanula lactiflora*: Among the best of this reasonably tall species are 'Prichard's Variety' (blue) and 'Loddon Anna' (pink).

Classic blue bellflowers pair well with pale roses

▶ *Campanula medium*: Canterbury bells is a biennial with very large single or double blooms in blue, pink or white. It looks well in cottage-style gardens. Pull up excess seedlings.

▶ *Campanula persicifolia*: The peach-leaf bellflower is soft powder blue, happy in sun or shade and along with its pure white counterpart, *C. p.* var. *alba*, seeds about inoffensively.

▶ *Dierama pulcherrimum*: In mild climates, angel's fishing rods, in pinks and purple-reds, steadily establish at the front of borders, their arching stems adding a carefree note.

▶ *Galtonia candicans*: The fragrant summer hyacinth has tall stems of waxy white bells, like giant snowdrops. A delightful addition to a border featuring roses.

▶ *Hemerocallis*: Day lilies come in a wide range of colours, sizes and flower forms, each bloom lasting around a day. Some yellows in particular, such as 'Hyperion', are fragrant.

▶ Lily: Modern cultivars for general border use are typically shorter and more robust than their older counterparts, with pretty doubles as well as singles in a wide range of shades – perfect for colour scheming. The tall white *Lilium regale* combines beautifully with old-style roses.

Pure white lilies combine well with peach roses

▶ *Nectaroscordum siculum*: The Sicilian honey garlic, flowers early- to mid-summer and its subtly shaded clusters of hanging bells provide a neutral foil for any rose. Attractive seed heads.

Roses growing amongst *Alchemilla mollis*, lady's mantle

▶ *Penstemon*: 'Andenken an Friedrich Hahn' (syn. 'Garnet') has deep ruby flowers; 'Schoenholzeri' (syn. 'Firebird') carries a profusion of small red blooms. The dark purple 'Blackbird' and 'Raven' have larger blooms on taller stems lasting well into autumn.

Froth and Mist

Several plants have a gauzy look and combine to romantic effect with roses. Others have plume-like flowers or see-through stems and almost floating heads that add a lightness when used in combination with the bold foliage and flowers. Lady's mantle and catmint are regularly used to edge traditional rose borders.

141

▶ *Alchemilla mollis*: Few country or cottage gardens would be without the acid-green froth of lady's mantle – the perfect foil for roses. Its pleated leaves capture rain in sparkling droplets. Deadhead before seeds set to prevent nuisance seeding.

▶ *Aster ericoides*: Now reclassified as *Symphyotrichum ericoides*, these autumn gems carry sprays of tiny daisy flowers, perfect for late roses. Try 'Pink Cloud' and the white 'Gold Spray'.

▶ *Crambe cordifolia*: Like a giant gypsophila, this early- to mid-summer flowering perennial makes a large mound of leaves topped by a giant branched flower head of tiny white honey-scented blooms – a magnet for insects.

▶ *Gaura lindheimeri*: Blooms of the white-flowered 'Whirling Butterflies' appear to hover in the air. A long-flowering front-of-border plant with autumn leaf colour.

▶ *Gypsophila*: Baby's breath is a favourite of florists everywhere. Grow *Gypsophila paniculata* 'Bristol Fairy' (double white to 1.2 m/4 ft) mid-border and *G.* 'Rosenschleier' (single pink) at the front. Avoid acidic or poorly drained soil. Cut back for repeat flowering.

▶ *Knautia macedonica*: The form 'Melton Pastels' (1.2 m/ 4 ft) carries scores of small pincushion flowers like tiny scabious on airy branched stems in pink and purple shades. Easy from seed. Avoid dry soils.

▶ *Macleaya*: Plume poppy is strikingly architectural, with lacy-edged leaves and tall feathery plumes with a buff tint.

R. 'The Fairy' growing with *Gypsophila* 'Rosenschleier'

In *M. microcarpa* 'Kelway's Coral Plume', the amber is pronounced and works well with roses in the same colour family, as well as creams and lilacs. Spreading.

▶ *Nepeta*: Amongst several excellent forms are catmint (*N.* × *faassenii*), in which felines love to roll, and its larger cousin 'Six Hills Giant', best fronting large shrub roses and Hybrid Teas. For smaller roses, try the neater *N. racemosa* 'Walker's Low'.

▶ *Stipa gigantea*: Golden oats is an evergreen grass with a low tussock of narrow dark green leaves topped by tall arching flower stems carrying cascades of shimmering flowers.

▶ *Thalictrum delavayi*: The airy branched flower heads of meadow rue are reminiscent of a tall gypsophila with maidenhair fern leaves. The tiny pendant blooms are lilac with cream stamens. The pure white *T. d.* 'Album' lights up in shade. 'Hewitt's Double' is lilac.

▶ *Verbena bonariensis*: The 'see-through' stems of purpletop vervain mean that it can be planted or allowed to self-sow through a border from front to back. The domed heads are violet-purple and a magnet for bees and butterflies. It may not overwinter, but often self-seeds.

Catmint (*Nepeta*) with *R.* 'Charles Austin'

Top Tip

Catmint (*Nepeta* × *faassenii*) is generous flowering, but can look a bit worn out after the first flush. When this happens, rejuvenate plants by shearing over (that is, taking a pair of shears or pruners and roughly chopping everything down to near ground level), watering and applying a liquid feed. Some vigorous repeat-flowering cranesbills (*Geranium*) also respond well to this treatment.

143

Spheres

The drumstick alliums that flower in late spring and early summer catch the first rose flushes and Old Garden roses perfectly. Their blooms range from magenta-purple through mauve to silvery-lilac and white. The large spherical heads of agapanthus appear mid- to late summer. Another blue at this time is the statuesque *Echinops* or globe thistle.

▶ *Agapanthus*: The African lily excels in frost-free gardens, but good, moderately hardy and free-flowering blues include 'Loch Hope', 'Brilliant Blue' and 'Jack's Blue'. 'Enigma' is palest blue to white and 'Arctic Star' pure white. Requires full sun, well-drained soil and summer moisture.

Roses and *Allium stipitatum* 'Mount Everest'

Echinops
bannaticus 'Taplow
Blue'

▶ *Allium*: One of the best of the many drumstick types is 'Purple Sensation'. 'Purple Rain' blooms a little later. *A. christophii* has very large silvery-lilac blooms on shorter stems and 'Mount Everest' is pure white. Attractive seed heads.

▶ *Echinops*: The globe thistle *Echinops bannaticus* 'Taplow Blue' has spiky balls on top of silver-white stems. *Echinops ritro* heads are soft grey-blue, while 'Veitch's Blue' is darker. Insect magnet preferring full sun and drainage.

▶ *Dahlia*: Pompom and ball types of this tender, tuberous rooted perennial have almost spherical heads in a wide range of colours. They flower all summer and into autumn if deadheaded. Fashionable dark crimson and purple reds include 'Cornel' and 'Moor Place'.

144

Cups and Bowls

The hardy cranesbills are classic rose companions and the sumptuous early-summer blooms of peony and oriental poppy add a romantic touch to mixed borders in period and country-house gardens. There are numerous anemones, but the Japanese types are an invaluable foil for the second main flush of bush roses.

► *Anemone*: Flowering in late summer and autumn, Japanese *Anemone* × *hybrida* cultivars have maple-like leaves and clear vertical stems topped with blooms. Try the tall white *A.* × *hybrida* 'Honorine Jobert', soft pink 'September Charm' and semi-double pink 'Queen Charlotte' ('Königin Charlotte'). The new *Anemone* 'Wild Swan' is a single white, blooming summer into autumn given moisture-retentive soil.

Anemone × hybrida 'September Charm'

► *Geranium* (cranesbill): There are many good blue selections for sunny or lightly shaded borders. Try the vigorous Rozanne; Orion (an improvement over the old variety 'Johnson's Blue') and the self-seeding pale-blue *G. pratense* 'Mrs Kendall Clark'. Geranium 'Mavis Simpson' is a free-flowering pink and 'Patricia' a vivid magenta with a dark eye. With low-growing Patio roses, try the pale pink *G. sanguineum* var. *striatum*.

► *Paeonia* (peony): Try the anemone-centred pink and cream 'Bowl of Beauty', singles such as 'White Wings' and doubles including 'Coral Charm' and the white 'Duchesse de Nemours'.

Oriental Poppy 'Patty's Plum'

► *Papaver* Oriental Group: Oriental poppies in strident reds with black centres such as the tall 'Beauty of Livermere' or the compact 'Allegro' predominate, but there are pretty pastel pink and purple shades, such as the New York series. For a ruffled light orange, try 'Aglaja'. Whites include 'Royal Wedding' and 'Perry's White'. 'Patty's Plum' is dusky purple. Cut back after flowering for a possible second flush.

145

Top Tip

Add instant colour to a rose-filled border that is between flower flushes by setting black pots filled with showy seasonal blooms directly on the soil between plants. Good candidates include tall grasses in flower such as the tender purple fountain grass (*Pennisetum* × *advena* 'Rubrum'); dark-leafed dahlias; species (wild) and hybrid lilies; *Salvia* 'Amistad', marguerite daisy (below) and fuchsias.

Daisies

Daisies have a carefree quality and are reminiscent of the wild daisies of the fields and countryside. The flower form works especially well with roses.

▶ *Anthemis*: For a very pale yellow, choose *Anthemis tinctoria* 'Sauce Hollandaise', a prolific bloomer for the front of a border.

▶ *Aster*: The soft blue aster hybrid *A.* × *frikartii* 'Mönch' is very long-flowering, disease-resistant and doesn't require staking.

▶ *Echinacea* (purple coneflower): *Echinacea* now has many unusual colour forms, but the rich pink *E. purpurea* and the amber-centred 'White Swan' are most reliable. Needs fertile soil.

Echinacea with roses

▶ *Leucanthemum*: Double white Shasta daisies include *L. × superbum* 'Wirral Supreme' and 'Aglaia'. 'Phyllis Smith' is single with twisted petals. 'Banana Cream', 'Broadway Lights' and 'Goldfinch' are soft yellow. Deadhead.

▶ *Rudbeckia* (black-eyed Susan): For moisture-retentive borders, the golden yellow *R. fulgida* var. *sullivantii* 'Goldsturm' will flower continuously through the growing season and is a good partner for scarlet, orange and cerise roses.

Leucanthemum × superbum 'Aglaia'

Plates, Domes and Umbrellas

The umbrella-shaped heads of certain culinary herbs and perennials add a wild, country feel to mixed plantings. The architectural forms of some, such as the purple angelica and steely sea holly, contrasts well with the relaxed ruffled blooms of shrub and groundcover roses.

R. 'Teasing Georgia' with Achillea millefolium 'Paprika'

▶ *Achillea*: Pastel-shaded yarrows include the soft yellow *Achillea millefolium* 'Moonshine', *A. m.* 'Lilac Beauty' and *A.* 'Salmon Beauty' (syn. 'Lachsschönheit'). For more vibrant oranges and crimson reds, try 'Walther Funcke' and 'Paprika'.

▶ *Angelica gigas*: Purple angelica is a giant of a plant with dark maroon purple stems, leaves and domed blooms. It is a short-lived perennial, flowering in its second year from seed. Blooms early- to mid-summer. Ornamental seed heads.

▶ *Chaerophyllum hirsutum* 'Roseum': Pink cow parsley flowers from late spring to early summer with gauzy lilac-pink blooms perfect for partnering old shrub roses in a country setting.

Angelica gigas

147

▶ *Foeniculum vulgare* 'Purpureum': The herb bronze fennel has diaphanous purple-tinged foliage and tall stems topped with flat plates of yellow. It is not showy, but is a wonderful foil for large roses.

▶ *Lychnis chalcedonica*: On good moisture-retentive soils, the scarlet red domes of Maltese cross top upright stems with fresh green leaves all summer long (90 cm/3 ft).

Top Tip

For a splash of late colour in mixed or shrub borders, plant crimson flag *Hesperantha coccinea* 'Fenland Daybreak' (syn. *Schizostylis*), which produces its coral-pink blooms into winter. Also try the autumn-flowering bulb *Nerine bowdenii* at the front of a sunny, drained border.

Vintage country feel – including Euphorbia, French lavender, lady's mantle, lupins, rosemary and lamb's ears

▶ *Sedum* 'Autumn Joy': Now *Hylotelephium* Herbstfreude Group, this bee and butterfly magnet provides front-of-border colour and a foil for late roses. *Hylotelephium* 'Matrona' has dark bronze-purple leaves and stems. Cut out one in three stems in late spring for more compact growth.

Vintage Blooms

The character of some perennials and biennials makes them the perfect fit for cottage and country-style borders featuring old-style roses. Traditional herb garden plants and any with silvery or grey foliage work well as a foil for crimson, pink, apricot and white roses.

▶ **Silvers and greys:** The gentle colouring of catmints (*Nepeta*), silver-filigree leafed artemisias and felted lamb's ears

(*Stachys byzantina*) combine with fragrant border pinks (*Dianthus*) for a period feel. The self-seeding rose campion (*Lychnis coronaria*) with vivid carmine blooms adds a pop of colour. Sea holly relatives like *Eryngium* × *zabelii* 'Big Blue' provide long-lasting metallic-blue thimble heads with a ruff of spines. The taller biennial *E. giganteum* (Miss Wilmott's Ghost) has silvery bracts (specialized leaves).

▶ **Cottage classics:** Along with cranesbills (*Geranium*), early-flowering bearded iris, such as the pale blue *Iris* 'Jane Phillips', work well in pastel schemes. If your soil is heavier, try the grassy leafed *Iris sibirica* in blues or purples. For more vibrant schemes, include *Geum* varieties in reds, oranges and yellows, as well as the later daisy-flowered *Helenium* cultivars and *Inula* species.

▶ **Perfume blends:** In late spring and early summer, blend the perfumes of biennial wallflowers (*Erysimum*) and later sweet william (*Dianthus barbatus*) with violas, pinks and roses. Late summer border phlox also have a heady scent and wide range of colours.

Gap Filling With Annuals

Hardy annuals, as well as half-hardy annuals that need some initial heat to germinate, can be used to fill holes in mixed borders. Good candidates have the look of a perennial. Make repeat sowings of

R. 'Scepter'd Isle' with magenta rose campion (*Lychnis coronaria*)

Top Tip

The many and varied evergreen *Heuchera* and × *Heucherella* cultivars make ideal foliage additions for rose gardens and mixed borders. Plant in groups towards the front of borders or singly in containers on the patio. In full sun, try the black-purple *Heuchera* Licorice or 'Obsidian'.

149

hardy annuals directly in the border (mid-spring to early summer) to ensure a succession of blooms. Alternatively, sow into divided seed trays and put the young plantlets where needed.

Try some of these annuals if you have gaps you want to fill:

- ▶ *Ammi majus*: Also known as bullwort
- ▶ *Antirrhinum*: Snapdragon
- ▶ *Calendula officinalis*: Pot marigold
- ▶ *Centaurea cyanus*: Cornflower
- ▶ *Consolida ambigua*: Larkspur
- ▶ *Cosmos bipinnatus*: Garden or common cosmos
- ▶ *Helianthus debilis* 'Vanilla Ice': Sunflower
- ▶ *Lavatera trimestris*: Annual tree mallow
- ▶ *Nicotiana* 'Lime Green': Tobacco plant
- ▶ *Nigella damascena*: Love-in-a-mist
- ▶ *Rudbeckia hirta*: Black-eyed Susan

Roses with larkspur (*Consolida ambigua*)

Roses with love-in-a-mist (*Nigella damascena*)

Top Tip

Plant winter- and spring-flowering bulbs to fill bare ground towards the front of mixed and shrub borders. Good candidates with rose bushes include dwarf bulbs like snowdrops (*Galanthus*), crocus species and *Crocus chrysanthus* cultivars, scillas and dwarf daffodils such as *Narcissus* 'Tête à Tête'.

The Shrub Border

Shrub borders are currently having a revival, with gardeners enjoying the advantages of reduced maintenance and year-round interest. Modern easy-care shrub roses, with their long flowering season and frequent bonus of colourful hips, make good additions.

Summer Flowers

Summer-flowering shrubs needing similar conditions to roses and that have contrasting flower and leaf forms are exemplified by the showy *Hydrangea paniculata* cultivars. Their cone-shaped heads typically start white and mature to pink by autumn. Early summer partners, happy on clay soils, include *Weigela*, *Deutzia* and *Philadelphus*. Potentillas meanwhile are invaluable, flowering all summer long with a range of colours. 'Primrose Beauty' and 'Limelight' are soft yellow.

Suitable shrubs to partner your roses include the following:

- ▶ *Buddleja davidii*: The aptly named butterfly bush
- ▶ *Buddleja* × *weyeriana* 'Moonlight'
- ▶ *Choisya* × *dewitteana* 'Aztec Pearl'
- ▶ *Choisya ternata*: Mexican orange blossom is fragrant
- ▶ *Deutzia*: White and pink shades
- ▶ *Escallonia* 'Apple Blossom': Profusion of tiny pink blooms
- ▶ *Hydrangea arborescens* 'Annabelle': Large domed heads
- ▶ *Hydrangea paniculata*: Mainly whites, 'Limelight' is green

Roses and lavender

151

▶ *Lavandula*: Try compact English lavenders like 'Hidcote'

▶ *Lavatera × clementii* 'Rosea': Abundant sugar pink blooms

▶ *Lavatera × clementii* 'Barnsley': White with a pink eye

▶ *Phlomis fruticosa*: Also known as Jerusalem sage

▶ *Potentilla fruticosa*: The shrubby cinquefoil is a prolific bloomer

▶ *Viburnum opulus* 'Roseum': Also known as the snowball tree

▶ *Weigela* cultivars: Crimson red, pinks, whites

Weigela praecox

Late Show

As summer turns into autumn and repeat-flowering roses produce a flush of late blooms and hips, borders take on a different personality. Fiery autumn foliage tints enhance late cream, red and orange roses, and hydrangea blues and purples, together with those of *Caryopteris* and *Perovskia*, add to the richness.

To extend your floral display, try some of the following:

▶ *Caryopteris × clandonensis* 'Heavenly Blue': Also known as bluebeard

▶ *Fuchsia*: Hardy bush forms bloom in rich cerise and purples

▶ *Hydrangea macrophylla*: Mop-head and lace-cap types

▶ *Hydrangea serrata:* Forms and hybrids include *H.* 'Preziosa'

▶ *Hypericum × inodorum* Magical series: For a range of berry colours

▶ *Perovskia* 'Blue Spire': Also known as Russian sage

Caryopteris × clandonensis 'Heavenly Blue'

Evergreen Colour

Country garden with path flanked with *Alchemilla mollis*, roses, hostas and *Choisya ternata* 'Sundance' trimmed to shape

In sheltered sites or milder regions, colourful evergreen shrubs light up the winter border as well as providing a colour-coordinated backdrop for blooms in summer. For instance, the pink- and cream-splashed *Photinia* 'Pink Marble' makes a pretty foil for the tall pink rose 'Queen Elizabeth'.

Try one of these for year-round interest:

▶ *Abelia* × *grandiflora* 'Kaleidoscope': Yellow and pink splashed

▶ *Abelia* × *g.* 'Francis Mason'

▶ *Choisya ternata* 'Sundance': Lime green to yellow

▶ *Elaeagnus* × *submacrophylla* 'Limelight': Yellow splashed leaves

▶ *Escallonia laevis* 'Gold Brian' and 'Gold Ellen'

▶ *Euonymus fortunei* Emerald Gaiety: White variegated

▶ *Ilex crenata* Golden Gem

▶ *Loropetalum chinense* var. *rubrum* 'Fire Dance': Purple-red, suits mild, frost-free areas

▶ *Nandina domestica* cultivars: Also known as Chinese sacred bamboo, fiery tints

▶ *Osmanthus heterophyllus*: For example 'Goshiki', cream and amber splashed

Top Tip

One group of shrubs that bridges the winter gap is *Viburnum*. Dot them through larger mixed or shrub borders for early fragrance and colour. Try the spreading *Viburnum farreri* (syn. *fragrans*) or upright *V.* × *bodnantense* 'Dawn' for fragrant winter blooms, and for mid- to late spring, the semi-evergreen *Viburnum* × *burkwoodii* 'Anne Russell' or compact deciduous *V. carlesii* 'Diana' continue to scent the air.

153

- *Photinia × fraseri* 'Red Robin' and 'Little Red Robin': Red new growth
- *Photinia × fraseri* 'Pink Marble': White and pink splashed
- *Pittosporum tenuifolium* 'Irene Patterson': White marbled
- *Pittosporum tenuifolium* 'Abbotsbury Gold'
- *Pittosporum tenuifolium* 'Tom Thumb': Glossy maroon

Photinia × fraseri 'Red Robin'

Foliage Effects

Deciduous shrubs are often faster-growing and more cold-tolerant than evergreens. Deep purple foliage works particularly well with most rose shades. Use gold or cream-variegated foliage to lighten dark groupings or as a foil for yellow and pastel shades.

Roses with *Sambucus nigra* f. *porphyrophylla* 'Black Lace'

For a seasonal display of foliage, try the following:

- *Cotinus coggygria* 'Royal Purple' and 'Grace': Also known as smoke bush
- *Physocarpus opulifolius* 'Dart's Gold': Also known as eastern ninebark
- *Physocarpus opulifolius* 'Lady in Red': Purple with red tints
- *Physocarpus opulifolius* 'Diabolo': Black-purple
- *Sambucus nigra* f. *porphyrophylla* 'Eva' (syn. 'Black Lace'): Also known as elder
- *Weigela* 'Florida Variegata': Yellow and cream variegated
- *Weigela florida* 'Foliis Purpureis': Purple leafed

Climbers and Wall Shrubs

Teaming a climbing rose with another climber or wall shrub makes it possible to extend the flowering season, before or after the main flush of the rose. You can also create some pretty colour combinations – a yellow rose and a soft blue clematis like 'Perle d'Azur', for example.

Roses and Clematis

The key to success is pairing the right vigour and flowering time of clematis with an appropriate rose. There are a number of options, and both roses and clematis enjoy the same conditions.

▶ **Dainty early birds:** Combine modern repeat-flowering climbers with mid-spring blooming *Clematis alpina* or *C. macropetala* and their varieties and cultivars. The ferny foliage will never overwhelm the rose and the clematis fills the spring and early summer gap.

▶ **Show stoppers:** Clematis in the early, large-flowered group, such as the favourite 'Nelly Moser', initially bloom in late spring or early summer on last year's stems and repeat in the autumn. They

155

only need light pruning after the first flush and work well with roses 2.4–3.6 m (8–12 ft) high. Meanwhile, the late, large-flowered group, including the purple *C.* 'Jackmanii', cope well with vigorous roses such as 'New Dawn'. Cut back in late winter to 30 cm (12 in) from ground level.

▶ **Small but numerous:** Clematis in the *Viticella* group, such as the carmine-red 'Madame Jullia Correvon', or in the Texensis group, such as 'Princess Diana' (pink bells), bloom mid-summer through till autumn on stems made in the same year. Cut back to 30 cm (12 in) in late winter. *Viticella* types often have the vigour to climb up Ramblers, providing a follow-on display.

A rose with *Clematis* 'Nelly Moser'

Getting the Blues

Large evergreen Californian lilacs (*Ceanothus*), with their vivid blue blooms, make a fine backdrop for late spring- and early summer-flowering roses in sunny borders. The deciduous 'Gloire de Versailles' blooms all summer and works well in a cottage or country garden. To partner a vigorous rose on a house wall, try the Chilian potato tree, *Solanum crispum* 'Glasnevin'.

The blue of Ceanothus goes beautifully with the yellow of *R. banksiae* 'Lutea'

Top Tip

To maximize fragrance on a large pergola or walkway in addition to perfumed roses, plant the late Dutch honeysuckle *Lonicera periclymenum* 'Serotina', common jasmine (*Jasminum officinale*), or a named fragrant wisteria cultivar – *W. floribunda* 'Kokuryu' (syn. 'Royal Purple'), for example.

Checklist

▶ **Edging and preferred partners:** Perennials traditionally used to edge rose beds include lady's mantle (*Alchemilla mollis*) and catmint (*Nepeta* × *faassenii*). Classic companions are cranesbills, pinks, bellflowers, foxgloves and delphiniums.

▶ **Contrasting habit and shape:** As roses tend to be spreading or arching, vertical forms create contrast – for example conifers, grasses and perennials with columnar or upright form. Marry roses with differing blooms, such as funnel-, bell-, cup- or bowl-shaped, spherical, tapering, flat or umbrella-shaped, frothy or daisy-headed.

▶ **Compatibility:** Ensure plant partners enjoy the same conditions as roses and that flowering coincides or overlaps. For early season colour beneath roses, plant snowdrops, crocus and scillas.

▶ **Gaps:** Fill spaces in mixed borders with annuals, biennials, summer bulbs and tubers that look like herbaceous perennials, such as dahlias, Canterbury bells and cosmos.

▶ **Vintage:** Old Garden roses and their lookalikes work well with silver and grey foliage and plants with soft blue or purple blooms; try herbs, cottage and country classics.

▶ **Shrub border:** Extend seasonal interest beyond rose flowering with evergreens and pick shrubs with complementary flower form or for foliage effects.

▶ **Climbing roses:** Team with another climber or wall shrub, choosing plants with similar size and vigour, growing and pruning needs.

Buying
& Planting
Roses

What and When to Buy

You can purchase roses through the year, but the cost per plant varies according to the type you request. It is traditional and cheaper to buy and plant roses in the winter, but gardening practices have changed and you can now plant at any time, weather and availability permitting.

Traditional Field-grown Roses

Roses are typically grown in fields using a technique called 'budding' (also known more generally as grafting). With this method, a tiny part of the rose one wants to propagate (including a bud and some surrounding tissue) is inserted into a slit made in the stem of the host rose (or 'rootstock'). The wild rootstock rose is cut hard back to allow the budded rose to grow without competition. There are pros and cons to budded roses:

▶ **Cheaper plants:** Field-grown budded roses can be distributed for planting in the dormant period, as bare-root or root-wrapped plants without soil, making transport cheaper.

▶ **Stress free:** There are fewer stresses on bare-root plants in winter and spring, as the soil is moist whilst they are establishing their root system.

▶ **More advanced:** The young field-grown budded roses may be better established than container-grown plants.

▶ **Limited availability:** Bare-root roses can only be lifted from the field and planted in the winter dormant period between late autumn and early spring.

▶ **On the clock:** Once bare-root roses arrive, you have a limited amount of time to get them planted.

▶ **Wait time:** If you want to give roses as a gift at a specific time of year, for a birthday or anniversary, for example, you may prefer to buy container-grown plants in bloom.

A bud grafted into rootstock

▶ **Reversion:** Particularly if improperly planted, the rose may revert to the wild rootstock.

▶ **Ongoing issue:** During the life of your rose, you always have to watch for reversions (stems of the rootstock coming up from the base) if it has been budded or grafted.

Containerized Roses

In winter, commercial nurseries pot up a quantity of their field-grown crop to sell through the rest of the year. There will be more choice of these roses if you order or buy earlier in the season, as supplies are limited.

Roses From Cuttings

The other main way that roses are sold is as container-grown rooted cuttings.

Own-root Roses

Some growers also plant little rooted cuttings directly in the field, which are lifted like bare-root roses once established. It is not surprising that these non-grafted roses are known as 'own-root' roses. One of the advantages of own-root roses is that they never suffer from reversions.

Rugosa roses are usually grown on their own roots

Best Time to Plant

In a warm or temperate region, you can plant roses at any time, avoiding periods of extreme heat or drought. Winter planting, when the roses are virtually dormant and concentrating their energy on their roots, is better for establishment. There is also less aftercare involved. In cold regions, there might be too much snow cover for planting in winter and the ground could be frozen solid. In these situations, it is better to plant in spring or early summer, but you may need to water more.

Sourcing Roses

There are so many ways to find roses now, you are almost spoiled for choice. You can buy them from specialist rose nurseries as well as companies growing a whole host of different plants or hedging. Garden centres invariably have a rose selection, and you can even buy from supermarkets in the bare-root season, though only buy if you know they have just been delivered. More and more people are now sourcing roses via the internet.

Ordering

Nursery catalogues and internet websites usually have a lot of detail and good photos. The information on the labels of garden centre plants is improving too. But if you get a chance to visit a rose nursery with gardens or fields open to the public when plants are in bloom, you can see at first hand what your intended purchase will look like once it has settled in.

▶ **Advance booking:** Try to order as soon as possible, as certain varieties will run out more quickly than others.

▶ **Personal collection:** You can sometimes arrange to pick up plants ordered through a nursery or garden centre if you live fairly locally, rather than pay delivery or postage costs.

Check for black spot

▶ **Mail order:** Items such as carefully packaged bare-root roses and hedging could be delivered at any time in the window specified by the nursery. Try not to order plants that might arrive whilst you are away.

Checking Plants

If you are buying plants directly, take time to look them over carefully. Also, when roses arrive by mail order, do not leave them in their packaging. Check them immediately for damage or signs of dehydration.

Here are some of the things you should be checking for:

Top Tip

If bare-root roses arrive and you are not able to plant them straight away, find a sheltered spot and dig a hole deep enough to put them in with the soil loosely backfilled to cover the bud or graft union by several centimetres. This is called 'heeling in'. If the ground is frozen solid, partially bury the plants in a large tub filled with moist potting compost and keep in a cool garage or frost-free building.

▶ **Health:** Check for pests and diseases like black spot, rust or mildew when buying plants in leaf. Don't be seduced by the flowers.

▶ **Breakages and damage:** With bare-root plants, check that the graft or bud union is secure (the graft/bud union is the point at which the grafted rose bud joins the rootstock – look for the lumpy bit between the shoots and the roots). Nurseries temporarily cover the union with tape or even wax, which may still be present. Reject plants with lots of broken roots or signs of shrivelling.

▶ **Overall shape:** Roses should have a good distribution of strong, healthy branches. Stems on bare-root and containerized bush roses in winter and spring will come ready trimmed or pruned, but may need some tidying up with secateurs at planting time.

Tools and Materials

The tools and sundries needed for rose planting and growing are not that different to those needed for cultivating other types of shrubs or for general gardening. One vital piece of equipment is a good-quality pair of bypass secateurs. You can do a lot of damage to roses with blunt pruners!

Bypass secateurs (as opposed to 'anvil' secateurs)

Equipment Check

Before planting, make sure that you have all the right tools to hand, especially if you have quite a lot of ground preparation to take care of before you can plant. When planting climbing roses, you may also need to attach the rose stems to structures and supports. This is what you will need:

▶ Digging fork and spade
▶ Border fork and spade
▶ Soil rake
▶ Thorn-proof gloves
▶ Secateurs
▶ Watering can
▶ Bamboo canes
▶ Bucket or builder's rubble trug
▶ String line and tape measure (if you want to lay roses out in a straight line).

Top Tip

If training climbers and Ramblers up on to walls, you can provide invisible support using vine eyes and horizontal wires set at 30–45 cm (12–18 in) intervals. You will need a drill, wall plugs, vine eyes, galvanized training wire and a tape measure, plus wire cutters and pliers to manipulate the stiff wire.

165

Planting in the Ground

The techniques for planting in beds and borders in the garden are a little different to planting in containers or raised beds. Good soil preparation is essential for the continued success of your roses, and careful planting increases the chances of rapid establishment and reduces potential problems in the coming season.

Avoid planting in frosty weather

Planting Weather

You are not always left with many options when it comes to planting roses in an unseasonably cold or wet winter, or in the height of a particularly dry and hot summer. But in general, follow these guidelines:

▶ **Avoid very wet periods** when clay soils especially could be temporarily waterlogged or prone to being damaged by cultivation. Planting in very free-draining soils will not be a problem.

▶ **Never plant in frosty weather** or if the ground is frozen. You may be able to scrape off surface snow and plant, provided the ground beneath is not frozen.

▶ **Avoid digging in summer**, especially dry, clay-rich soils, as this can damage the soil structure. Try to avoid planting in drought conditions or extreme heat, as you may not be able to provide sufficient water to allow the new plants to establish.

Weeding and Soil Preparation

Before planting, ensure that the soil is free from weeds and reasonably friable (crumbling consistency, not solid). Prepare as follows, but do not over-cultivate the soil:

▶ **Digging:** Dig over a wider area than required just for planting the rose. Use a digging fork or spade to roughly break up the soil to just below fork or spade depth. This ensures that the roots have access to a wider area of soil than just the planting hole and reduces potential waterlogging in clay.

▶ **Weeding:** As you cultivate, pick out roots of perennial weeds and pull up annual weeds. In wild garden areas and when planting shrub roses in long grass, clear a circle of at least 1 m (3 ft) in diameter.

▶ **Soil improvement:** On free-draining, poor and stony soils, lightly fork manure or well-rotted garden compost into the general planting area. If you do not have any to hand, apply a general-purpose fertilizer as a base dressing (that is, mixed into the soil rather than as a top dressing).

Soak the roots of bare-root roses before planting

Adding mycorrhizal root grow to the roots

Preparing Bare-root Plants

The main thing to ensure is that the plants have not been out of the ground too long or stored somewhere warm such as inside a shop. Bare-root plants usually arrive with their roots wrapped in plastic. In garden centres and nurseries, they may be offered for sale outdoors in winter, temporarily potted up in relatively small but deep pots.

▶ **Keep covered:** Only unwrap bare-root roses and hedging just before you plan to plant. It is essential that the roots be kept moist and not left out on the ground to dry out in sun and wind.

▶ **Soak:** Shortly before planting, soak the roots in a large bucket or trug, especially if there are signs of dehydration. Just 30–60 minutes should be sufficient.

▶ **Lightly trim:** Only if absolutely necessary, trim off any obviously damaged or broken roots and cut back branches that have been only roughly trimmed by the nursery, to just above a bud.

▶ **Mycorrhizal treatment:** Particularly on poor ground, not previously improved with generous helpings of manure or compost, you may want to consider mycorrhizal fungi 'root grow' product. Holding the rose over the planting hole, dust the root system using a freshly opened sachet of mycorrhizal product. Do not use granular fertilizer at the same time, as it interferes with the fungus.

Did You Know?

Naturally occurring mycorrhizal fungi provide a vital service to plants, connecting their roots to a much greater volume of soil via a microscopic network of fungal threads. These facilitate the transfer of nutrients to the plant roots, and some growers consider extra mycorrhizal treatments especially helpful when establishing new roses. Roses sometimes have difficulty obtaining enough of the right nutrients, especially on poor soils or where roses have previously been grown (*see* page 89).

Preparing Container-grown Plants

Plants purchased in containers may be in full leaf and even in bud or flower. Do not worry if you are not quite ready to plant. They have enough food in the compost to sustain them for several weeks, provided you continue to water them. Before planting container-grown roses:

▶ **Plunge into water:** Fill a deep container with water and plunge the whole of the pot into it, submerging the compost surface, and wait for the stream of air bubbles to stop. This ensures that water has penetrated to the core of the root system – a place that's hard to reach with only a watering can!

▶ **Do not disturb:** Carefully remove the pot, but do not attempt to tease out the roots, as this can cause damage.

169

Planting in Borders

Make the hole twice the width of the plant and dig the hole deep enough for the graft union to sit at or slightly above soil level. For container-grown plants, the final depth should be the same as the surface of the compost, but double-check where the graft union sits.

Follow these steps when planting:

Add well-rotted manure or compost

▶ **Manure:** Put about a spade full of well-rotted manure or garden compost in the bottom of the hole and fork into the base, loosening the soil there to allow excess water to drain through.

▶ **Finding the level:** Lay a bamboo cane across the hole to lie at the original height of the border surface and use it to help determine the correct planting level.

▶ **Root space:** With bare-root roses, spread out the roots as evenly as possible in the hole and holding the plant at the right level with one hand – using the cane as a guide – start to back fill with soil. Be careful not to leave large air pockets.

Finding the level

▶ **Correct depth:** With container-grown roses, ensure that they are not planted too deeply. Adjust the soil level accordingly. Equally, do not plant with the surface of the root ball proud of the surrounding soil. This causes the top of the root system to dry out.

170

If necessary, dig out the hole more; do not draw soil up around the protruding root ball, as this will eventually wear away, leaving the top exposed.

► **Firm in:** Using your foot, lightly tread the soil around the edges of the planting hole so that the ground is pushed into contact with the roots. Level the surface again with a border fork or with your hands. On drier soils, it helps to leave a depressed ring around the plant, as this captures rainwater, directing it to the roots.

► **Watering:** Using a watering can with the rose (spray head) removed, water the area immediately round the plant to settle the soil in round the roots, and fill in any gaps. Each rose needs about a gallon-sized (4 litre) can of water.

Planting Climbers

The soil next to walls and fences is usually dry, due to something called the rain-shadow effect. The wall or fence effectively shields the ground around it from rain. Near walls, planting conditions can be made worse by shallow foundations and residual rubble, which should be removed.

Before planting climbing roses:

► **Enrichment:** Dig plenty of moisture-retentive manure or well-rotted homemade compost into the general planting area.

171

▶ **Avoid the rain shadow:** Dig the planting hole as described above, but set it around 45–60 cm (18–24 in) from the base of the wall or fence.

▶ **Angled planting:** Lie the roots or root ball in the hole at an angle so that the tip of the stems or cane support just touches the wall or fence. Back fill as described above and ensure that you do not leave the angled section of root ball exposed.

▶ **Support:** It may be necessary to cut the ties holding the rose branches to the support canes so that you can spread out the stems and, if necessary, re-attach them to a new set of canes. Fasten the stems or canes to the lower training wires with soft garden twine or stretchy/padded flex that will not cut into the rose as it grows.

Propagating Your Own Roses

Planting rose cuttings. It takes a year for them to root and be ready to dig up and move

Cheaply bulk up favourite roses from hardwood cuttings taken between mid-autumn and late winter (just as the roses are losing their leaves or just as they are coming into growth in late winter), using stems 15–30 cm (6–12 in) long, about pencil thickness, produced that year. Remove the soft tips and any leaves and cut just above a bud at the top and just below a bud at the base. Dip the base in fresh hormone rooting powder and insert in a trench of well-drained soil so that two thirds of the cutting is below ground and a third above. Leave till the following autumn before transplanting.

Planting Hedging

As well as the English shrub roses listed on pages 74–75, several compact Alba and Gallica roses, as well as numerous Modern shrub roses, can be used as hedging. You will need thick gloves to handle some of the species roses and their named forms, including the yellow-flowered Spinosissima hybrid 'Frühlingsgold', which makes a vigorous easy-care barrier for a wild or seaside garden. The Rugosa hybrids also thrive as coastal hedges.

Follow these directions when planting:

▶ **Marking out:** Use a taut string line to mark the hedge position and roughly dig over the whole length, turning over and weeding to a width of about 1 m (3 ft) and digging to a spade's depth.

▶ **Enrich:** Incorporate plenty of bulky organic matter in the form of well-rotted manure or garden compost. If the soil is particularly poor, apply a base dressing of general fertilizer along the length. Roses are hungry plants and a hedge may quickly run out of nutrients, being close-spaced.

173

▶ **Equal spacing:** Use a tape measure or marked cane to space the planting holes, so that the base of each plant is 45 cm (18 in) from the next. You can plant a little further apart for very dense and vigorous roses used in wild gardens.

▶ **Planting hole:** Dig and prepare the planting hole as described above and use a bamboo cane to check the plant is at the correct depth. Do not add fertilizer to the base of the hole (used in this way, today's granular or powdered fertilizer is just too concentrated and will burn the roots of the rose).

▶ **Finishing off:** Firm the hedge plants in well with your foot as described above and water thoroughly.

▶ **Mulching:** If possible, and only on top of properly moist ground, apply a deep mulch to conserve moisture (*see* pages 187–88).

Ensure that the planting holes are spaced at equal distance along the row.

Did You Know?

Native rose species make excellent additions to mixed wildlife hedges – for example, the dog rose, *Rosa canina*, and eglantine or sweet briar, *R. rubiginosa*. Such wild roses are valuable to pollinators, create habitat for birds and other animals and their hips are a good food source. When ordering bare-root country- or wild-mix hedging, be sure to specify some wild roses.

Planting in Containers and Raised Beds

A big change in the way we grow roses in gardens today has been the realization that most can be grown in pots and planters. This enables beautiful rose blooms to be included in places where there are no borders, such as patios and courtyards. The same care must be taken when planting, and it is worth remembering that roses in containers require regular watering and feeding, increasing your workload.

Containers

When selecting the right pot for your rose, bear in mind that you may need to re-pot into a larger container at some point, so avoid ones where the neck narrows at the top. The size should be large enough for the rose to look in proportion and to accommodate a few years' growth. Tall pots work well with bushy spreading roses and also give the long roots plenty of soil depth.

175

Here are some pot-picking pointers:

▶ **Drainage:** Check that the container has drainage holes at the bottom.

▶ **Soil depth:** Avoid relatively shallow or small containers and troughs unless planting miniature or small Patio roses or dwarf Polyantha types. Small pots mean more watering and restricted growth!

▶ **Insulated metal:** Avoid metal containers unless they have an insulating liner to protect the roots from extremes of heat or cold.

▶ **Stability:** Reconstituted stone or thick ceramic pots, as well as heavy wooden planters, are less likely to blow over in windy gardens.

▶ **Moisture loss:** Glazed ceramic pots keep moisture in the soil better than unglazed terracotta, which has a bearing on maintenance.

▶ **Weight restrictions:** Plastic or resin fibre pots are lightweight and suitable for balconies and roof terraces.

Planting Roses in Pots

To prepare the pot, you can cover the drainage holes with fine mesh or broken pot pieces (crocks), but do not

Adding a few crocks to help drainage is fine, but don't go overboard, as the roots need as much space as they can get!

176

fill the base with gravel (roses do much better when given as much compost as possible for their roots to grow into, and a deep gravel layer could restrict growth).

Prepare the roses, bare-root or container-grown, as described earlier and then plant in a good-quality weed-free loam compost with added nutrients, such as John Innes no. 3, mixing in around 10 or 20 per cent of a good-quality multi-purpose compost or well-rotted manure, which helps with moisture conservation. You could also add gel crystals (*see* page 192). Firm with your hands, leaving the finished soil level around 2.5 cm (1 in) below the rim to allow for watering.

Raised Beds

You can think of raised beds almost like giant containers. One advantage is that they lift smaller plants up to where their blooms and fragrance can be better appreciated. They work well round seating areas, as the plants come to around shoulder height. Though it is better for raised beds to have an open base directly on to soil, you can construct them on solid concrete, provided you make provision for drainage in the form of weep holes in brick and stonework.

Preparation and Planting

Fill raised beds to the very top with good-quality loam or soil, at the same time mixing in a proportion of well-rotted manure or garden compost. Some suppliers offer pre-mixed blends. The soil will gradually sink down, as it

177

is full of air pockets, so needs firming before you plant. If safe to do so, firming in large raised beds can be done by standing on the soil and gently treading it. You may need to add extra soil as it sinks.

It really is as simple as this:

▶ **Level:** Rake over the ground to level off the surface, ready for planting.

▶ **Planting holes:** Prepare the holes as you would for planting in a border.

▶ **Settle the soil:** Firm plants in with your hands.

▶ **Water:** Give each plant a good, long drink!

Top Tip

Add extra height to low raised beds by growing roses up wooden or wirework obelisks. English roses and Miniature Climbers are ideal.

Checklist

▶ **When to plant:** The winter dormant period is best, but in cold regions wait till the ground thaws.

▶ **Sourcing roses:** Buy from nurseries, hedging suppliers, garden centres, mail order and the internet.

▶ **Budded (grafted):** Traditionally, roses are budded on to field-grown wild-rose rootstock.

▶ **Own-root:** Rooted cuttings grown in containers or directly in the field do not suffer from reversions.

▶ **Bare-root:** Lifted only in winter, these are cheaper and establish more quickly with less aftercare than container-grown roses planted in the growing season.

▶ **Container-grown:** Plant any time, avoiding frost or drought. Soak thoroughly beforehand.

▶ **Planting in borders:** Make the planting hole twice as wide as the rose and a little deeper to allow for manure and the like to be mixed in. Plant to just at or below the graft union.

▶ **Hedges:** Use a measure or marked cane to space plants 45 cm (18 in) apart.

▶ **Climbers:** Plant 45–60 cm (18–24 in) away from the wall or fence and angle the stems back.

▶ **Propagating:** Plant cuttings in mid-autumn to late winter, to be ready for the following autumn.

▶ **Roses in containers:** Select large pots with drainage holes, in scale with the rose.

Caring for Your Roses

Recent Plantings

Your new treasures deserve the best start and there are several things that you can do to ensure they get it. It is a good idea to inspect roses regularly for several months after planting to check on their progress and spot any problems such as lack of water, or rabbit or wind damage.

When to Water

Although roses planted during the winter dormant period have fewer issues with moisture levels than roses planted in summer, a dry spring can slow down new growth and additional watering may be necessary to encourage shoot growth. It is worth remembering that newly planted roses do not yet have access to moisture like ones with a fully established root system.

Other reasons to water include:

▶ **Roses in leaf:** Container-grown roses planted out in borders during the growing season have greater demands on their small root systems, having to provide water to maintain existing foliage and flowers. Continue watering new roses for at least the first two summers.

182

▶ **Drought:** When rainfall is negligible, especially in conjunction with warm, windy weather, which increases moisture loss from the shoots, growth slows dramatically. Vulnerable new shoots, buds and leaves may shrivel and die back.

▶ **Free-draining soil:** By adding copious organic matter, such as manure, and by mulching when the soil is moist (*see* pages 187–88), you can greatly improve the moisture-holding capacity of free-draining soils, but you may still need to water new plantings whilst soil conditions are being improved.

▶ **Pots and containers:** Newly potted roses on a sunny patio are especially vulnerable to drying out and may have to be watered daily, at least until properly established.

How to Water Efficiently

Roots should be encouraged to work their way down through the soil to seek out moisture. Frequent light watering does the opposite and roots end up near the surface and vulnerable to heat and drying out.

Here are some tips on how to use water wisely where it will do most good:

▶ **Water in the cool:** If watering is necessary between mid-spring and mid-autumn, do it in the early morning or in the evenings. This reduces wastage through evaporation.

183

▶ **Long drink:** Water newly planted roses in leaf once every three or four days in their first summer, gradually extending to weekly waterings if weather permits. Give the rose enough water to penetrate well down into the soil, rather than regularly sprinkling the surface. Dig down to check how deep the water has gone if you are not sure – around 45 cm (18 in) is ideal.

▶ **Keep it low:** Avoid splashing water on the stems and foliage, as this can spread black spot.

▶ **Easy access:** A porous or perforated hosepipe is ideal for laying along the length of a recently planted hedge. The gentle trickle seeps well down into the soil profile instead of running off.

▶ **Watering moat:** Create a moat, mounding the soil around the rose to keep irrigation water close to the root zone. This is especially important on sloping ground.

▶ **Roses in pots:** Put a shallow dish or pot saucer under each container to catch water run-off.

Attraction to Animals

In more rural areas, animals such as rabbits may target new plantings, especially in periods where natural food is scarce. They may eventually lose interest, especially as the season progresses and more food is available. *See* pages 213–14 for deterrents.

184

Windy Gardens

Gusts and gales are capable of causing a lot of damage, especially to newly planted shrubs that have not got their roots down properly. Roots act like an anchor once established. Constant wind strips moisture from foliage and shoot tips, causing leaves to 'burn' or shrivel, and the situation is made worse if salt spray is involved on coastal sites. In windy gardens, you may need to stake plants or provide temporary shelter for new rose plantings.

Here are some tips to help protect your plantings from the wind:

▶ **Wind scorch:** Protect newly planted hedges or individual roses using a permeable barrier of windbreak mesh that reduces the strength of the airflow. Drive in temporary stakes at regular intervals on the windward side and attach the mesh with a heavy-duty staple gun. Alternatively, use heavy-duty, transparent plastic tree guards.

▶ **Wind rock:** Plants can be blown over or loosened in the ground, a process called wind rock. Check new plantings regularly and use your foot to firm the soil back round the stems of affected plants, gently pulling them upright. Wind rock prevents the roots from establishing properly, and it may be necessary to use a short stake and rose tie to stop the plant moving around at the base.

▶ **Lighten the load:** Prune top-heavy shrubs on planting to reduce the sail effect in windy gardens.

185

▶ **Climbers:** Regularly tie in new growth on more vigorous climbers, as the stems can be damaged if unsupported and left to flail around in the wind.

Weeds

Weeds often come up as a rash of seedlings when soil is disturbed at planting time, and with extra watering and fresh nutrients, can quickly grow and create problems. Weeds and lawn grass compete for water and foodstuffs and sometimes for light and root space if they get really big.

What to watch for when weeding:

▶ **Annual weeds:** Clear weeds by hand to avoid damaging surface roots.

▶ **Perennial weeds:** Keep watch for perennial weeds and tree seedlings, whose root systems are harder to dislodge if allowed to grow for any length of time. Carefully dig down to expose the weed root and try to remove it all.

▶ **Mulching:** Prevent new weed growth by applying a mulch (*see* opposite).

Feeding and Mulching

Roses, like any flowering shrub, respond well to plentiful food and moisture during the growing season. There are all kinds of ways to feed roses effectively, including granular or liquid rose feeds and foliar feeds that are sprayed directly on to the leaves. If you have easy access to horse manure and somewhere to store it covered with a tarpaulin to let it rot down properly, this can provide some but not all of the necessary nutrients when dug in or applied as a mulch.

Benefits of Mulching

A thick mulch of well-rotted manure, garden compost, local authority green waste (broken down in a compost digester to be free of weed seeds) or ground, composted bark helps to seal in soil moisture and prevent weeds. As it rots down and is incorporated by earthworms, some nutrients are also released. Avoid spent mushroom compost, as roses prefer a slightly acidic soil to allow them to take up nutrients effectively and this contains chalk/lime.

Did You Know?

Organic mulches gradually break down and need to be kept topped up to be effective. The soil underneath the mulch improves in structure over time, and on clay that means better drainage in winter and less cracking in dry weather. Free-draining sandy soils hang on to moisture and nutrients better with regular mulches of organic matter, especially manure.

How and When to Mulch

Apply a layer of mulch at least 7.5–10 cm (3–4 in) thick in early spring when the ground is moist. Keep the mulch a few centimetres away from the neck of the rose or its stems, as the moist material can cause the woody stems to rot. Top up as necessary. Only mulch moist ground, never frozen.

Feed and Fertilizers

Roses, like all flowering shrubs, require nitrogen (chemical symbol N) for leaf and shoot growth, phosphorus (P) for roots, and potassium (K) for flower and hip production. On every packet of fertilizer, you will see the N:P:K ratio, which lets you know the proportions of each. Specialist rose fertilizers and some other good general feeds also add trace elements and minerals.

When to Feed

Fertilizer should be applied twice a year, following the instructions on the packet or bottle. Particularly in areas experiencing cold winters, do not feed garden roses again after the second mid-summer feed, as this can make growth too soft to withstand frost and winter temperatures. Roses hard pruned annually require more feed than those given a light trim. Keep the following in mind when deciding when to feed:

▶ **Early spring:** Feed as soon as you see the new leaf and shoot buds start to develop after winter dormancy.

▶ **Cold regions:** It takes plants a little longer to get growing, so delay the first feed until mid-spring.

Top Tip

When applying bark mulch or wood chip mulch in early spring to control weeds, first sprinkle a top dressing of general-purpose granular fertilizer. Wood takes nitrogen from the soil and plants as it starts to rot down, and the fertilizer compensates for this initial loss. As it decomposes, wood mulch eventually releases nutrients back into the soil. Do not worry if you see a white fibrous fungus in the mulch. This is perfectly harmless.

▶ **Poor, sandy soil:** Applying a general fertilizer around pruned bush roses might be better on these soils for the first feed, as plants might need a little more nitrogen to kick-start growth. In very wet seasons, fertilizer can be washed down out of the root zone and repeat-flowering roses may need an interim feed to keep them blooming.

▶ **Rose fertilizer:** Use a granular rose fertilizer or a good-quality sustained-release fertilizer with trace elements. Repeat again mid-summer after the first main flush.

189

▶ **Tomato feed:** In cold regions, around the time you would normally apply the second feed of rose fertilizer, consider swapping it for tomato feed, which is rich in potassium and helps toughen up growth ready for winter.

Feeding Roses in Pots

Apply a granular rose fertilizer or quality sustained- or slow-release fertilizer with added trace elements as a top dressing (that is, on top of the soil) in spring. Be careful not to get this on the plant. This will keep the rose growing strongly and producing flower buds, but a liquid rose feed or a foliar feed, which is sprayed on to the leaves, will be valuable for additional flower encouragement later in the growing season. Stop feeding at the end of the late summer period.

Top Tip

Beware of over-feeding roses. Too much fertilizer can make rose growth too soft to overwinter and shoots become more susceptible to pests and diseases. Too much nitrogen causes lots of soft sappy and leafy growth at the expense of blooms.

Top Tip

Every other spring, before applying fertilizer, scrape off loose soil and mulch from the top of the pot and replace it with fresh compost mix. Mulch the surface again after watering.

Watering

On moisture-retentive soil, and if spring and summer rainfall is plentiful, you may not need to water roses planted in the ground after the first couple of summers. However, in areas with dry, free-draining soil or a Mediterranean climate with relatively dry summers and high temperatures, watering may have to be part of the gardening routine.

Reducing Watering

Cut down the need for watering by using deep mulches applied on moist ground in spring and by using more drought-tolerant types of rose that may only need infrequent deep summer waterings once established. Drought-tolerant roses include:

▶ Native roses
▶ Albas (for example 'Königin von Dänemark')
▶ Gallicas (some, for example 'Tuscany Superb')
▶ Tea roses
▶ Noisettes
▶ China roses
▶ Hybrid Musks
▶ Polyanthas
▶ Rugosa (species and hybrids)
▶ Ramblers
▶ Bourbons (some, for example the climbing 'Souvenir de la Malmaison')

R. 'Tuscany Superb' is a drought-tolerant rose

191

Roses in Containers

Roses in patio pots and planters require regular watering to thrive, and in summer this can mean daily watering.

Here are some ideas to help reduce watering:

Top Tip

Remove pot saucers for winter, as the compost needs to drain and not retain excess water.

▶ **Gel crystals:** Incorporate water-retaining gel crystals/granules in the potting mix at planting time.

▶ **Mulch for moisture:** Use moisture-retentive organic mulches like manure on top of the compost.

▶ **Catch the drips:** In summer, stand pots on saucers to catch water that runs through.

▶ **Group pots:** This makes watering easier, especially when pots are clustered near an outside tap or water butt.

▶ **Automated watering:** Install a drip-feed automatic watering system to your outside tap and consider an automated timer so that pots can still be watered if you are away. Check the nozzles occasionally, as you may need to adjust.

Roses in Borders

Most repeat-flowering bush and shrub roses, as well as rose hedges, should only need watering once a month in summer. You may also need to water in spring if the weather has been dry after the roses start actively growing. Follow the general instructions on page 183 for 'How to Water Efficiently'. Climbing roses need more regular attention if they are in the dry shelter of a wall or fence.

Flower Power

Repeat-flowering bush roses, including Floribundas, Hybrid Tea, Patio, Miniature roses and large-flowered English shrub roses, produce a lot of blooms over a long period. These benefit from regular deadheading to encourage more flowers and to improve the appearance of the plant. Hybrid Musk roses and Old Garden roses such as Portlands with larger blooms also respond well. Once-blooming roses and some shrub roses may not need anything more than a tidy up at the end of their flowering season.

Deadheading

Depending on the size of bloom and whether they are carried singly or in clusters, use a pair of bypass (not anvil) secateurs or smaller flower scissors to deadhead.

▶ **Large single blooms:** Remove the faded bloom, cutting back down to just above a bud. Rather than leave long, leafless stems, prune back to where there are side shoots and leafy growth.

▶ **Cluster-flowered:** Remove individual flowers in a cluster as they fade and, when all have finished, cut back the head and its stem to leafy growth and side shoots. This combines deadheading and light pruning.

▶ **Hip production:** Wild roses and many single or semi-double flowered shrub roses often have attractive displays of hips. Most of these do not need or benefit from deadheading. However, if the shrub repeats, you could deadhead early on but leave the last flushes to produce fruit.

193

An Introduction to Simple Pruning

Roses do not need to be pruned except to remove dead wood, which can be done at any time of year. We gardeners prune to control the shape and size of plants and the position of the flowers. Some shrub roses and climbers get very tall and threadbare at the base over time, and selecting a few of the oldest stems to cut out or shorten brings the flowers down to eye level and causes the base to fill out.

Tools and Sundries

You will need a good-quality pair of bypass secateurs. Do not use anvil types, as they crush the stems when cutting. The general rule for choosing the right cutting tool is, if you cannot cut through stems cleanly in one go with secateurs, you should be using bypass loppers or a small, foldaway pruning saw.

Here are the pruning tools you will require:

▶ Bypass secateurs
▶ Pruning saw
▶ Bypass loppers
▶ Hedging shears
▶ Thorn-proof gloves
▶ Hedge-trimmer (optional)

Pruning saw, bypass loppers and bypass secateurs

Top Tip

Do not prune during a drought, as it puts unnecessary
stress on the rose as it tries to re-grow.

General Pruning Pointers

An easy way to remember the basics that apply to all roses is to think of the four Ds – remove or cut back Diseased or Damaged stems, cut out Dead wood and prune beyond brown Dieback into healthy white pith. Finally, deal with Defective material, including suckers (*see* page 219), or branches that are overlong compared to the rest, pointing in the wrong direction or which are rubbing against another branch.

With the great variety of roses, there is variance in the ways they should be pruned. Here is a quick guide:

195

▶ **Early blooming Old Garden roses:** These flower from older wood produced in previous years. They need very little pruning, and care must be taken to maintain their graceful shape. On established shrubs, take out a few of the oldest stems at the base, concentrating on those causing congestion. Prune after flowering in mid- to late summer.

Did You Know?

It is not necessary to prune to a bud that is pointing in a specific direction, as roses do not always respond in the way you expect. Similarly, do not make the traditional angled cuts: straight cuts leave less exposed tissue and reduce the chances of infection. Simply cut to within 0.63 cm (¼ in) above a bud to minimize the risk of dieback.

▶ **Repeat-flowering bush roses:** These Modern roses are generally hard pruned in late winter or early spring by about a third to a half. In very mild climates, prune in mid-winter. These flower on the current season's growth and how hard you prune depends on the plant's vigour and how big you want to let it grow. Applies to Hybrid Teas, Floribundas, Patio and Miniature roses.

▶ **Standard roses:** Various rose types, including Polyantha, Floribunda, Patio roses and low-spreading shrubs, can be grafted at the top of a long stem grown from the rootstock. Prune the heads according to the grafted rose type and try to maintain the same balanced shape as the original.

196

▶ **Groundcover roses:** Vigorous repeat-flowering shrubs, landscape or groundcover roses can be cut back in late winter using hedging shears or even an electric hedge-trimmer.

▶ **English roses and repeat-flowering shrubs:** Established plants have last year's growth cut back by about a third and side shoots shortened to two or three buds from their origin. Every few years, take out a small proportion of the oldest stems at the base.

▶ **Polyantha roses:** These are obliging, low-maintenance roses that could be cut fairly hard like Floribundas, sacrificing earlier blooms, or simply be left alone except for deadheading and the basic pruning of the 4Ds.

Did You Know?

If you move into a new garden and inherit an old tangled and overgrown shrub or climber, you can revive it. The hard pruning to restore its shape and encourage new wood is done in the winter dormant period. You may lose a couple of season's flowers.

▶ **Ramblers:** These mostly bloom once on wood produced the previous year and require little pruning except to control their vigour. Pruning after flowering is done in late summer.

Top Tip

In cold regions, wait until mid-spring to prune roses normally tackled in late winter.

Modern Climbers

Pruning is done to encourage new growth to spring from the main supporting stems (canes) and their side branches (laterals). The short side shoots bearing the blooms are known as flowering spurs.

A couple of things to bear in mind when pruning climbers:

▶ **Build a framework:** Pruning and training is carried out in late winter or early spring with the aim of building up a spaced-out framework of near-horizontal main branches tied to wires or on to a frame (*see below*). Do not prune back the main canes until they have covered the space or, for example, finished covering an archway.

▶ **Established plants:** Cut one or two older canes out at the base to encourage leaves and flowers lower down. Cut back flowered laterals by about two thirds and shorten the canes by a third to a half to encourage side shoots. Remove surplus stems.

Training for More Blooms

The closer that the stems of climber or shrub roses are to the horizontal, and the more you stress them by bending them down and round, the more flowers they produce. The Victorians were experts in the art of training roses. Use soft garden twine or stretchy/padded flex to gently but firmly hold the stems in place. Train in late winter, taking care when bending stems, as the less pliable may snap.

Training on Walls

Ramblers, the yellow banksia rose, tender Noisettes and other old roses, like the robust and shade-tolerant Albas, can be trained on wires and the stems allowed to cascade down walls, creating a sumptuous arching effect. With very long pliable canes, you can bend them round and back on themselves, attaching to the horizontal wire below.

Training Over Frames

Robust ironwork tripods, domes and open square frames are ideal for supporting large shrub roses. Train old roses, such as *Rosa* 'Tuscany Superb' or *R.* 'William Lobb', up through the frame to cascade down. Large Modern Shrubs, such as 'Dortmund', 'Felicia', 'Marguerite Hilling' or the vigorous English rose 'Constance Spry', also benefit.

Pillars and Obelisks

These come in varying sizes. For best flower production, rather than simply tying the climber's stems to the support vertically, wind the stem round starting from the base, creating a series of slightly angled turns. This is an excellent way to train Miniature Climbers.

Top Tips

To attach rose stems, tie twine onto the wire first and knot, before looping the ends round the stem and tying back to the wire.

R. 'Constance Spry' works well trained on frames

Checklist

▶ **Watering:** During establishment, water every few days. Once established, water in the first two springs and summers, unless very wet. If dry, water fortnightly, especially on light soils and for climbers.

▶ **Weeding:** Hand weed to prevent competition.

▶ **Wind protection:** Check new plantings for wind rock and firm in. Consider staking or using a windbreak.

▶ **Roses in pots:** Use pot saucers in summer. Top dress in spring with rose feed and later with liquid or foliar feeds. Mulch. Consider drip irrigation.

▶ **Feeding:** Apply rose or slow-release fertilizer in early spring (later in cold regions) and again mid-summer.

▶ **Mulching:** Apply a deep layer of well-rotted organics over damp soil in early spring to reduce watering, feeding and weeding.

▶ **Deadheading:** Remove faded flowers of semi-double and double roses. For hips, leave later flushes.

▶ **Pruning:** Use correct tools to remove dead, diseased, damaged or defective stems. Cut down bush roses by a third to a half in early spring, English roses more lightly. Prune once-blooming roses lightly in mid- to late summer after flowering. For climbers, create a horizontal framework of long stems, reduce laterals and remove unwanted growth.

▶ **Training:** Bending stems to a horizontal position or lower stimulates flowering.

Pests & Problems

Cold, Heat and Humidity

The best way to ensure that your roses are healthy and trouble-free is to choose varieties that enjoy your climate. Black spot, a fungus that vexes growers in areas with mild, wet summers, is not a problem in Mediterranean or desert climates, but roses there need to be heat-tolerant. Cold plays havoc with more tender roses, but there are superb cold-hardy equivalents.

R. 'The Queen Elizabeth' is cold-hardy

Cold-hardy Roses

Most roses happily go dormant in winter, but severe cold can kill plants outright or cause dieback. Winter winds add to the pressure, causing moisture loss.

Cold-tolerant roses include:

▶ **Old Garden roses:** Albas and Gallicas are very hardy, as is the Moss rose 'William Lobb'.

▶ **The Queen Elizabeth:** This tall Floribunda/Grandiflora is hardy to -28°C (-18.4°F).

The Modern Climber *R.* 'Golden Showers' bears up well in the cold

▶ **Species roses and hybrids:** This group contains several wild roses plus the robust *Rosa rugosa* and Scots rose (*R. spinosissima*) hybrids.

▶ **English roses:** Some are particularly hardy, such as 'Crown Princess Margareta', 'A Shropshire Lad', 'Susan Williams-Ellis' and 'Gertrude Jekyll'.

▶ **Modern Climbers:** Several climbers have a tough constitution, including 'Altissimo', 'Golden Showers', 'Compassion' and 'Aloha'.

▶ **North Americans:** The exceptionally hardy Canadian Explorer, Parkland and Buck series (*see* page 77) are a must for cold-climate gardens. Also try the resilient Knock Out® roses.

Preparing for Winter

For cold-climate regions where roses go completely dormant, follow these suggestions:

▶ **Tidy:** Do not prune, but remove dead flower heads and pick off remaining leaves, removing any that have fallen.

▶ **Soil mound:** Bury the rose base by mounding up the surrounding soil.

Mounding up the surrounding soil provides insulation in cold climates

205

One way to insulate is by wrapping with horticultural fleece

▶ **Mulch:** Apply a deep layer of bark chips or similar free-draining material.

▶ **Insulate:** For very cold weather, insulation can be key. Try covering shorter plants with an open-ended box, fill with dry material such as packaging chips, close and weigh it down to stop it blowing away. Alternatively, wrap with several layers of horticultural fleece. Tie taller stems together before insulating.

▶ **Extreme solution:** Dig a trench and loosen the roots on one side to enable you to lean the rose over and bury it in the soil. Cover with more dry mulch.

Winter Container Care

In cold regions, or when the temperatures drop lower than normal for your region, provide temporary shelter for patio pots by moving them to the base of a warm and sheltered wall. Large heavy pots and ones with wall-trained climbers must be wrapped *in situ*.

Other precautions you might take in the event of very cold weather include:

▶ **Drainage:** Remove saucers to avoid compost becoming too wet. Raise pots on 'feet'.

▶ **Fleece wrap:** Wind layers of horticultural fleece around the stems, securing with twine. This allows air and light through, preventing moisture build-up.

Top Tip

In areas with cold, dry winters, water rose roots thoroughly in autumn to ensure that they are not drought-stressed.

206

▶ **Standard roses:** As well as wrapping the head in fleece, use plumbers' pipe insulation to protect the highly vulnerable stem. If frost penetrates, the sap expands and splits the bark.

▶ **Root protection:** Rose roots in pots are vulnerable to freezing. Wind several layers of bubble wrap around the pot. Alternatively, use thick layers of straw or dry bracken, covered with hessian fabric tied with rough twine.

Roses for Hot, Dry Climates

Given irrigation, many roses excel in a Mediterranean climate. Even in desert regions, some roses cope with heat, though blooms will not last as long and colours may fade. Erecting temporary netting provides overhead shade. Roses go dormant in high temperatures. Black spot is minimal due to low rainfall.

If you garden in a warm climate, try:

▶ **Tea roses:** These include the copper pink double 'Général Schablikine', pale buff 'Safrano' and apricot yellow 'Climbing Lady Hillingdon'.

▶ **China roses:** Fortune's Double Yellow (*R. x odorata* ' Pseudindica') is a large shrub or climber with semi-double pale yellow-pink blooms. 'Cramoisi Supérieur' is short-growing, crimson pink, semi-double.

▶ **Bourbons:** The fragrant pink climbers 'Madame Isaac Péreire' and 'Zéphirine Drouhin' are both heat-tolerant. Ensure plentiful soil moisture.

207

▶ **English roses:** Good varieties include the compact crimson-purple 'Darcey Bussell', white 'Lichfield Angel', double pink 'The Alnwick Rose' and yellow 'Molineux'.

▶ **Hybrid Teas and Floribundas:** Experiment with tender varieties of both and seek out fragrance, such as the double apricot, dark-leafed Floribunda 'Lady Marmalade'.

▶ **Modern Climbers:** Some resilient cultivars include 'Golden Showers' and 'Don Juan', the latter an Italian cultivar from the 1950s with fragrant, crimson double blooms. Repeats. Humidity tolerant.

R. 'Lichfield Angel' is an English rose that works in hot climates

The Modern Climber *R.* 'Don Juan' can tolerate hot, dry weather

Roses for Humid Regions

Fortunately there are roses that cope well in these conditions and breeding work and trials continue to find roses that thrive in the tropics and other humid regions such as Louisiana and South Florida.

▶ **Old Garden roses:** The Noisettes, mainly tall repeat-flowering shrubs or climbers in yellows and pastel shades producing large clusters of blooms, all seem to do well. For varieties, *see* page 55–56. The Tea rose 'Duchesse de Brabant' also obliges.

Top Tip

Some roses listed above would be suitable for the dry south-east of England. *See also* pages 89–90 and 191 for drought-tolerant roses.

▶ **Brindabella roses:** A varied group of roses, including many Hybrid Teas, some bred by the Brindabella Gardens, these mainly perfumed roses have been trialled in Queensland, Australia and found to be heat- and black spot-resistant. All are tolerant of the humid east coast climate. They include the *R. persica* hybrids 'Eyes for You' and 'For Your Eyes Only'.

▶ **English roses:** Try 'Pat Austin' (coppery orange-yellow), 'Evelyn' (pale apricot), 'Heritage' (light, clear pink), 'Molineux' (yellow), 'Abraham Darby' (apricot pink), 'Princess Alexandra of Kent' (rich pink) and 'Windermere' (creamy white).

▶ **Bush and groundcover roses:** Try the orange Floribunda 'Easy Does It', the lilac pink Hybrid Tea 'Belinda's Dream' (an Earth-Kind® rose; *see* below) and groundcover roses in the Drift series.

Earth-Kind® Roses

Horticulturists at Texas A&M University trialled 468 roses growing without fertilizer, spraying or pruning (except for dead wood). They had no extra watering after their first year. The original winners, with more being added, are known as Earth-Kind® roses due to their having minimal impact through cultivation or chemical use. Once established, they are heat- and drought-resistant. Varieties include several Polyantha and repeat-flowering shrub roses.

The groundcover rose 'Easy Does It' thrives in humid conditions

Did You Know?

The Indian rose breeder Viru Viraraghavan has been working to produce a new series of tropical climate roses based on crossing *Rosa clinophylla*, found on islands in the Ganges river, and the yellow form of *R. gigantea* (Northeast India, Northern Myanmar and China's Yunnan province).

209

Rose Diseases

Happy, vigorous-growing roses that are well cared for are far more able to avoid or fight off disease. Always select disease-resistant forms and look out for Earth-Kind® roses.

Black Spot

The common fungal disease black spot is unsightly, but except in very bad seasons with warm, wet weather, doesn't harm the rose unduly. Telltale yellow patches followed by black spots on the leaves appear, causing badly affected leaves to fall. Fungicides are available, but may not be required if you choose resistant varieties and break the fungal cycle.

Black spot

Other ways to combat black spot include:

▶ **Dry leaves:** Avoid evening watering and keep water off foliage.

▶ **Pruning:** Hard-prune bush roses in early spring, removing much of the overwintering fungus.

▶ **Mulch:** Apply a mulch immediately after pruning or top up existing mulches.

210

Powdery mildew

▶ **Late leaves:** Pick off all remaining leaves from plants in winter and any that have fallen.

▶ **Compost ban:** Do not compost rose leaves or prunings.

Other Diseases

Several other diseases affect roses, and can be more severe in certain environments. Always look for resistant varieties, maintain good airflow and keep plants growing strongly.

Here are some of the diseases to which roses are prone:

▶ **Rose mildews:** There are two types. Downy mildew coats the undersides of leaves with off-white mould, and upper sides are yellow blotched. Powdery mildew coats affected shoots, leaves and buds with white 'powder' and can cause dieback and leaf-fall. It is worse in drought conditions. Clean debris underneath roses. Water only in the mornings and keep it off foliage. Fungicides are available.

▶ **Botrytis:** In cool, damp weather, especially in autumn and in still air, buds and flowers may become infected with botrytis or grey mould fungus. It leaves them shrivelled and covered in a grey down. Cut off affected parts.

Botrytis

211

▶ **Rose rust:** Symptoms include dusty orange fungus spots on the undersides of leaves, turning brown in summer. Leaves drop and the fungus overwinters on the rose stems and in debris. Grow rust-resistant roses like 'Fragrant Cloud' and 'Sexy Rexy'. Fungicides are available.

▶ **Virus:** Aphids and other sapsuckers can introduce viruses, for which there is no cure. Affected plants show yellow flecking or mottling and sometimes yellow veins and distorted leaves.

▶ **Honey fungus:** Roses are susceptible to this usually fatal disease that causes the whole or part of the plant to die off. A white fungal web forms under the bark, and sometimes honey-coloured 'mushrooms' appear in autumn. Dig up and destroy if the disease is confirmed.

▶ **Dieback:** This can be caused by the graft union being buried. In most cases, set it at ground level or slightly above. (In very cold regions, soil can be piled up to cover the base of the rose and graft union for insulation purposes before adding a dry mulch, but the soil and mulch should be removed in spring after the thaw.)

Rose rust

Did You Know?

There is increasing evidence that salvias (ornamental sage) such as 'Caradonna' and the showy New World cultivars like 'Amistad' and shrubby *Salvia microphylla* types, such as 'Cerro Potosí' (deep pink), 'Jezebel' (cherry-red) and the red and white 'Hot Lips', may stave off fungal diseases such as mildew and black spot. Ornamental alliums, chives and other onion family members, especially garlic, have long been used for dual pest and disease protection.

Dealing With Pests

You cannot stop creatures attacking garden plants, but there is much you can achieve by creating a balanced natural environment that fosters insect predators. Physical barriers work best for larger animals.

Animal Pests

Plastic guards such as these may be required to protect young roses from rabbits

Two significant pests of roses in rural areas are rabbits and deer. It can be a very costly business building a barrier right round your plot. Protecting individual plants is more practical.

Rabbits

These not only nibble at the stems, but also undermine roses, digging at the roots. The problem is often worse in winter and early spring, when other food is scarce. Try:

▶ **Temporary barrier:** Surround affected plants with wire mesh held in place with bamboo canes.

▶ **Stem guards:** Where possible, fit spiral rabbit guards around stems, especially on vulnerable standard roses, to protect the bark. These wind on and should be pushed partway under the soil.

▶ **Tree guards:** Or try more heavy-duty 60-cm (2-ft) tall plastic tree guards to protect young hedging roses and climbers.

213

▶ **Chemical sprays:** There are numerous recipes for home deterrents as well as environmentally safe sprays sold in garden centres and DIY stores. But success varies, and you need to repeat treatments regularly, especially after rain.

Deer

Despite the thorns, deer happily graze on roses, finding the blooms a delicacy! Unless you have a deer-proof fence around your plot, if present locally, they will probably make a beeline for any new plantings. The options above for rabbits can work for deer too, or to protect larger individual shrub roses, surround with a timber and wire mesh barrier.

Did You Know?

There is always a lag between the build-up of aphids and the arrival of their natural predators, which delay breeding until there are sufficient aphid numbers to sustain their offspring. Wait a while before turning to insecticide sprays, as you risk wiping out the natural predator's food source and potentially killing these beneficial creatures.

Insect Pests

The pests that target roses vary around the world, but aphids (greenfly) are widespread. Frequently check your roses, concentrating on shoot tips, new foliage and flower buds, and turning leaves over to look at the undersides. A small hand lens is a useful aid. Several pests are only active at night, so you may need a torch.

Aphids

Green or pink aphids can occur in large numbers on shoot tips and flower buds in spring and summer. Aphids introduce viruses. Quick detection is key to preventing population explosions.

Here, you can see the white cast aphid skins (exoskeletons) as well as the green aphid

Here are the signs of aphids:

▶ **Distortion:** Shoots, leaves and flower buds pucker, twist and shrivel due to sap sucking.

▶ **Black mould:** Aphids secrete sticky honeydew, which becomes infected with black sooty mould. It is unsightly but washes off.

▶ **White remains:** Greenfly shed their skins, leaving white exoskeletons sometimes mistaken for whitefly.

Dealing with aphids:

▶ **Remove:** Rub off colonies with thumb and forefinger, blast them with a strong jet of water from a hosepipe or cut off badly infested shoot tips.

▶ **Natural enemies:** Aphids have plenty of natural enemies, including parasitic wasps, predatory midge larvae, ladybird (ladybug) beetles and larvae, hoverfly larvae and lacewing adults and larvae. Small insect-eating birds also feed on them. Allow these creatures to do their job.

▶ **Soap spray:** If cultivation remedies do not work, consider spraying the aphid colonies on the shoot tips with insecticidal soap. Avoid spraying in hot weather or drought conditions to prevent scorching.

Lacewings are natural predators of aphids

215

Japanese beetles are particularly a pest in North America

Rose sawfly larva

Rose leafhopper

Beetles

A range of beetles feed on roses, more commonly in the US, including rose bud borers, rose chafers and Japanese beetles. Hand pick or put a sheet under the bush and shake them off. Destroy by dropping into soapy water. Biological control is available to kill larvae in lawns.

Rose Sawfly Larvae

Some sawfly larvae roll the leaves to camouflage themselves, other species lay eggs into the stems. These caterpillars are small, green with yellow and black markings and have voracious appetites. Hand pick rolled leaves and cut off shoots with large numbers of larvae or hand pick individually.

Rose Slugworm

These small slug-like creatures on the backs of leaves are not slugs but the larvae of certain sawfly wasps that eat away tissue to leave skeletonized foliage. Pick off damaged leaves.

Rose Leafhopper

These insects feed on the undersides of leaves, causing the surface to be pale and mottled, especially in very sheltered spots. Pick off affected leaves and spray problem plants with a suitable insecticide.

Top Tip

Apply all pesticides and fungicides according to the manufacturer's instructions, taking all precautions and disposing of safely. Spray after pollinating insects are active, in summer not until the late evenings, at twilight.

Rose slugworm

A Green Approach

Minor holes and nibble marks can usually be ignored, and damage like the semi-circular holes made by leaf-cutter bees is transient and harmless. Minimize your use of chemicals, as these can have a detrimental effect on the predators of pests and other beneficial insects. Hand pick, rub off with thumb and forefinger or blast off insects with a strong water jet.

You can use the force of water to blast off insect pests

Avoiding Pests and Diseases Naturally

Here are some pointers for creating a generally healthy environment for roses:

▶ **Clean zone:** Keep the ground around the rose free from weeds, grass and debris.

▶ **Mulch barrier:** Mulching in early spring separates soil-borne pests and diseases from roses.

Inspecting your roses regularly enables you to catch pests and diseases early

▶ **Pick clean:** Clear up fallen rose leaves and prune out or pick off diseased material and infected leaves. This is especially important in autumn.

▶ **Compost exclusion:** Do not compost rose leaf litter or prunings, especially diseased material, as spores can survive and re-infect.

▶ **Airflow:** Space roses to allow good air circulation and maintain a gap between ornamental planting partners. Prune roses to reduce congestion.

▶ **Stress free:** Avoid stressing roses by cultivating them well, mulching and supplying adequate water and nutrients. Do not plant on waterlogged ground. Avoid lime-rich soils if possible (if you want to grow roses in chalk or limestone soils, at least avoid *R. rugosa* and hybrids, which are very sensitive).

▶ **Rose diet:** Do not overfeed roses, especially with nitrogen-rich fertilizers, as this encourages insect pests.

▶ **Water wise:** Water in the mornings to reduce night-time humidity, and avoid wetting stems and foliage unless blasting off insect pests with the hose.

▶ **Naturally resistant:** Plant disease-resistant roses and pick varieties suited to your local climate and soil conditions.

▶ **Gardeners' friends:** Encourage natural predators, providing food plants and habitat for adults and their larvae, such as ladybirds (ladybugs), hoverflies and lacewings.

▶ **Bird haven:** Encourage insect-eating birds by feeding, as well as creating cover and nesting places.

Most ladybirds are a welcome sight in any garden

Other Problems

R. 'Zephirine Drouhin' with suckers emerging from the ground

Aside from the more common pest and disease problems, there may be other factors affecting the health and appearance of your roses, some of which are outlined below.

Rose Suckers

On budded or grafted roses, sometimes shoots grow up from below the graft union. These belong to the wild rootstock and are quite different in appearance from the rest of the rose. Follow the stem to its origin, scraping away soil to see where it joins. Pull the sucker off cleanly to prevent it from growing back. Occasionally, a budded rose dies off, perhaps in a severe winter, leaving the wild rootstock to continue growing. At this point, it is best dug up and discarded.

Cultivation Issues

Some problems arise from poor cultivation practices or prevailing weather conditions. Examples include:

▶ **Root rot:** Roses hate poor drainage and waterlogged soils, especially in winter, and this can cause the roots to rot, killing the plant.

This rose shows signs of nutrient deficiency, in this case probably magnesium or iron

219

▶ **Rose replant disease:** Poor growth is seen on new roses planted in an area where they have previously been cultivated. This is not actually a disease, but a result of nutrients being stripped from the soil. Remove as large a volume of the original soil as possible, replacing with fresh loam and well-rotted manure, and try using a mycorrhizal treatment.

▶ **Nutrient deficiency:** Roses prefer slightly acidic soils. Rugosa hybrids especially show chlorosis (yellow leaves) on alkaline soils. Over-feeding with certain fertilizer and mulch combinations can also prevent uptake of nutrients – for example, too much tomato food rich in potassium can cause magnesium deficiency. This shows as yellow patches between the veins. If plants show magnesium deficiency, you can treat them with a foliar spray of diluted Epsom Salts (try 1 tablespoon of Epsom salts per 4 litres/1 gallon of water for each foot of the shrub's height). Treat in spring as leaves appear and then again after the roses bloom.

▶ **Weed-killer drift:** Take care with weed killers, as the spray can drift on the breeze and damage foliage, causing it to die back or become distorted.

Excess sun can scorch roses

▶ **Balling:** This bud problem occurs in shady, cool and damp conditions, where the outer petals, saturated with water, dry out. A stiff coat then forms and stops the bloom opening. Remove affected heads. Some varieties are more prone than others.

▶ **Rose ties and support wires:** Try to stop stems growing behind wire supports and trellises, as this leads to problems with congestion and access for pruning. Avoid using wire ties, as these can cut into wood as the stem expands.

▶ **Shade:** Four or more hours of good sunshine is ample for most modern roses. Less than that and some can stop flowering and become drawn. In hot Mediterranean or desert climates, afternoon shade prolongs flowering.

Checklist

▶ **Climate:** In hot climates, avoid problems with disease by choosing resistant and heat-tolerant forms. In cool climates, choose cold-hardy roses and protect and insulate plants in winter.

▶ **Green approach:** Give roses optimal growing conditions and promptly remove dead or diseased material and fallen leaves. Use early spring mulches. Opt for organic control methods.

▶ **Fungal diseases:** Select resistant varieties and ensure good air circulation.

▶ **Viruses:** These can be transmitted by aphids and other sapsuckers, so take measures to control their numbers.

▶ **Dieback and honey fungus:** Poor drainage and winter cold both cause dieback. Roses are also susceptible to honey fungus – remove the plant if infected.

▶ **Deer and rabbits:** Protect individual roses by using physical barriers.

▶ **Insects:** Watch for build-up on shoot tips, buds and leaves. Watch for rolled leaves. Blast off with water jets or rub/pick off manually. Try organic sprays and soft soap. Inspect plants regularly.

▶ **Natural pest predators:** Encourage these by providing them with food and habitat, including winter shelter; avoid chemical sprays.

▶ **Rootstock suckers:** Pull off suckers from below the graft union.

221

Taking Things Further

Fresh-cut Roses

There is something special about cutting roses from your own garden or allotment to use in your home or to give as a gift. Shop-bought roses tend to be rather uniform and sometimes lacking in character, and those in bunches of one variety are often Hybrid Teas with little fragrance. When you grow your own, you can pick favourites, ones with a rich fragrance or that open to a particularly beautiful form, such as some of the old roses.

The Cutting Garden

Having somewhere to grow flowers purely for cutting is an indulgence. The roses you select do not have to be good garden plants in terms of their overall shape and foliage cover. They can be quite gaunt and leggy, as long as the blooms appeal. You can grow any type of rose, because you are not bound by the constraints of commercial growers, who generally need plants with single blooms on long stems.

When planning your cutting garden, you may want to consider the following:

▶ **Rows:** Grow in straight lines to allow easier access for cutting and maintenance.

▶ **Blocks:** Include several of one variety, if possible, in order to give you sufficient numbers of the same rose when making up a bouquet.

▶ **Smooth stems:** Consider growing virtually thorn-free varieties.

▶ **Rose companions:** Remember, grow what you really like and include some frothy filler plants in toning, neutral or contrasting colours to mix with your roses.

How to Cut, Condition and Prepare Roses

Cut blooms in the cool and damp of early morning or in the evening. After the sun has gone down is a good time, as long as you can still see what you are doing! This lessens the stress on the flowers, as their cells will be full of water. If possible, have a deep bucket of water to hand, so that you can soak them as soon as you cut them.

Choose flowers that are just opening from bud

When harvesting your blooms, bear the following in mind:

▶ **Cutting:** Cut as long a stem as possible without damaging the plant or cutting off new buds. You will cut the stem shorter once it has been arranged in a bouquet or just as it is put into a vase.

▶ **In bud:** Select flowers that are just opening from bud and showing colour. If they are too young, they may not have the energy to open, while full-blown roses will soon start dropping their petals.

225

▶ **Condition:** Leave soaking in deep water in a cool, shady and sheltered spot for several hours before arranging. The warmer it is, the faster the blooms will open.

▶ **Good hygiene:** You can add flower-conditioning liquid, but it is not essential. It is more important to change the water regularly and use clean containers.

▶ **De-thorn:** Use a paring knife, nail clippers or a special thorn stripper to remove the thorns to make the roses easier to handle when arranging. This is optional. Take off lower leaves that will be submerged so that they do not foul the water.

Simple Hand-tied Bouquet

These can be as large or as small as you like, uniform circular posies or asymmetrical with one side longer.

Top Tip

Seal the cut ends of stems of plants that drip milky latex or coloured sap, such as euphorbia or poppy, in a flame before conditioning. This prevents them from wilting and fouling the water.

The idea is to create a base background of loose, frothy or lightweight flowers or foliage, using that as a support framework whilst you thread through larger blooms, such as your roses, from the top down. Lay all your materials out on a table in front of you.

Here is a step-by-step guide to creating a simple hand-tied bouquet:

▶ **Form the dome:** You will hold the developing bouquet in one hand and pick up your flowers with the other. Place each new stem at a slight angle so that you start to form a spiral. Create your support network or base using small-flowered or 'frothy' stems, such as a bright green euphorbia (take care with the sap which is an irritant) or *Alchemilla mollis* (lady's mantle).

▶ **Second tier:** Slot larger blooms with branching flower heads or perhaps flower spires through the frothy dome, spacing them out. Leave some sticking out above the dome for variety. Gather each new stem in with the rest.

▶ **Add roses:** Finally, add several larger blooms. Roses will be the main event, but you could also add one or two other flowers, such as contrasting coloured dahlias, carnations and so on. Keep turning the arrangement in your hand and pull from the base to shorten overlong stems.

▶ **Tie off:** Take a long piece of string that has already been folded in half. Lay it over the stems and pass the two loose ends through the loop and pull tight. Lay the bouquet down on the table and tie off as normal. Trim the stems level.

Easy Arrangements

Here are some simple tricks to help give your arrangements a professional look. Shallow containers are ideal for table settings because guests have an unobstructed view.

▶ **Shallow containers:** Use pre-lined shallow wooden boxes or glass or ceramic dishes filled with water.

▶ **Pre-cut roses:** Cut the rose stems so that each bud and short stem are the same length.

▶ **Pack together:** Fill the container with rose heads. Pack them together to hold each other up vertically.

▶ **Floral foam:** Alternatively, pre-soak a block of wet floral foam (such as Oasis) and cut to fit the container. Push in the stems.

Did You Know?

When roses are cut and brought indoors, their fragrance develops in the relatively warm and still air. You will notice this particularly if you have the door to the room shut and then re-enter some time later. Notes of citrus, tea or musk often become more apparent.

Buttonhole Rose

You do not have to have a lot of flowers in the garden to make a buttonhole: a single rose will suffice. Cut and condition your rose as described earlier, then cut the stem shorter, but allow for fixing as a buttonhole or to attach to a handbag. You can also use these tiny arrangements in a specimen vase or as part of gift-wrapping.

How to make your buttonhole rose:

▶ **Background froth:** Select a sprig or two of something with tiny blooms or a ferny leaf (this can be trimmed down if too large).

▶ **Make the buttonhole:** Remove any rose thorns and then put the fine-textured foliage or blossom behind the rose head, holding all the stems together.

▶ **Bind the stems:** Use fine florist's wire to hold the mini bouquet together and then wrap with green florist's tape so that the blooms are held firmly and the stems form a narrow stick.

229

Rose Crafts

Dried and pressed rose blooms and petals, as well as rose leaves, can be turned into lovely gifts, cards and pictures or decorations for the home. You can even make your own potpourri or natural confetti for a wedding.

Making Rose Confetti

A simple paper cone filled with rose petals is a lovely touch at a wedding, and you could stack the petal-filled cones in a basket to hand out to guests as they arrive. Petal confetti is not hard to make, but the process does take about two or three days. It can be speeded up using a catering desiccator or a very cool fan oven.

▶ **Petal production:** Only use unblemished petals gently pulled from each rose head.

▶ **Drying trays:** Lay out on trays covered with dry tea towels, cardboard or several layers of absorbent kitchen roll.

▶ **Warm atmosphere:** Place in a warm room with some ventilation or a large airing cupboard.

230

▶ **Ready for use:** Check the petals after a day or two. They should feel dry to the touch. Discard any that have gone brown.

▶ **Presentation:** Pack the petals into your handmade cones.

Did You Know?

Dried rose petals can be crushed up slightly into smaller pieces to make rose-scented potpourri. Pink and lilac roses dry to reds and purples, and red roses turn almost black-red when dried.

Drying Whole Roses

It does not matter what shade of rose you use for drying whole. It is worth experimenting to find your favourites, but red roses hide any blemishes well and are supremely romantic. On a dry day, around noon, pick roses that are newly opening and just out of bud stage. These are less likely to drop their petals as they dry.

Here are two simple and effective ways of drying whole roses:

▶ **A place for drying:** Put the cut stems spaced out into an empty container in a warm, airy room, but out of direct sunlight, which will fade the colour. Air-conditioned rooms are ideal, as the system extracts moisture from the air.

▶ **Drying line:** Another way to dry is to peg individual stems to hang upside-down from an indoor washing line.

How to Use Dried Roses

Once dried, roses can be arranged in a number of ways, but take care, as the petals will be brittle. These everlasting blooms will stay looking good for several years and can be mixed with other dry flowers for easy-care flower arrangements.

Here are just a few suggested uses:

▶ **A single rose:** Individual blooms can be given as a gift, tied with a piece of colour-coordinated gauzy wired ribbon.

▶ **A place setting:** A single ribbon-tied rose would also make a lovely place setting for a dinner party. Alternatively, use to add the finishing touch to a large gift-wrapped present.

▶ **Add a romantic touch:** Dried roses are perfect for a bedroom or bathroom, filling a small basket or attached to a mirror or picture frame, perhaps. Use a hot-glue gun from a craft supplier or thread through a frame of chicken wire packed with dried moss.

In the Kitchen

Roses have edible petals and, because of their fragrance and beautiful form, have many uses in flavouring, cooking and food decoration. Always ensure that you use roses from your own garden, or ones that you know have not been sprayed or treated with any kind of pesticide or fungicide. Rinse thoroughly before use.

Homemade Rose Water

You can make small quantities of rose water to use in a variety of ways for cosmetic and culinary use at home. The process requires a little care, and stringent selection of fresh, unblemished petals. Use highly fragrant pink or red roses if available, varieties of *Rosa rugosa* such as the deep pink 'Hansa' or

magenta-purple 'Roseraie de l'Haÿ', for example, and pick newly opened blooms very early in the morning to preserve as much fragrance as possible.

▶ **Harvesting your roses:** Gather the heads into a container and, if you prefer, pick off the petals indoors. Lightly rinse to remove any dirt or debris.

▶ **Prepare to heat:** Place in a large pan and just cover the petals with filtered water.

233

▶ **Simmer gently:** Avoid boiling the mixture, reducing the heat to a gentle simmer. Cover.

▶ **Colour transfer:** Heat in this way for 20–30 minutes, or until the petals have lost their darker red colour and are pale pink or almost colourless.

▶ **Natural cooling:** Leave to cool down completely with the lid on.

▶ **Separate:** Strain the liquor through muslin to produce the clear, pink rose water.

▶ **Frozen perfume:** Pour into ice-cube trays and freeze for later use. Seal the ice cubes in containers to prevent loss of perfume and defrost as necessary. You can also keep small quantities in sealed bottles in the fridge for about a week.

Top Tip

Use your rose-water ice cubes or freshly prepared rose water to flavour whipped cream or cake frosting/icing; or add to fruit punches, homemade cordials or other cold drinks. Also try it in muffin and sponge cake mixes for a delicate hint of rose.

Making Rose Petal Tea

Rose is known for its calming qualities and makes a pleasant alternative to other herbal teas. Dried rose tea is available, but you can make it from fresh rose petals. Gather a handful, rinse and add to a warmed teapot. Pour over boiling water and allow to steep for a while. A blend can be made with green tea if preferred.

Decorating Cakes and Desserts

There are numerous ways to decorate a large cake or smaller cup cakes using fresh or crystallized roses or rose petals for a really romantic touch. Or simply capture the feel of high summer during afternoon tea and scatter a few fresh petals on the tablecloth and around the tiers of a cake stand.

Did You Know?

You can scatter freshly rinsed rose petals in savoury salads to add colour and subtle flavouring.

Fresh Petals

For an easy but highly effective decoration, gently press fresh rose petals into a complete coating of buttercream applied with a palette knife. Space the petals randomly, but leave very few gaps. Palest pink petals or creamy gold would work well for a wedding cake.

Crystallized Blooms

Use individual crystallized rose petals or rose buds to decorate cup cakes or handmade biscuits. Stick on with icing, frosting or a swirl of buttercream or cream. Do not forget to use rose-flavoured sugar as one of the cake or frosting ingredients (*see* page 237). To prepare, pick the buds and petals, gently rinse in a sieve (sifter) and dry on absorbent kitchen paper.

Did You Know?

You can use rose leaves as a stencil on top of a plain Victoria sponge cake or lemon tart. Place the leaves and then sift fine icing sugar from a sieve to cover the cake. Carefully remove the leaves, leaving your design.

235

Then simply follow these few steps:

▶ **Egg white:** Separate an egg, setting aside the yolk to use in cooking later.

▶ **Lay out:** Space the buds and petals out on a wire cooling rack or on baking trays covered with waxed kitchen paper.

▶ **Egg white coat:** Select an artist's paintbrush and coat the bud or petal with egg white. You may have to pick them up to paint the reverse.

▶ **Buds:** Tiny rose buds just showing petal colour crystallize relatively quickly. Try Polyantha rose varieties like 'The Fairy'.

▶ **Sugar coat:** Using finely sieved (sifted) caster (superfine) sugar, shake the sugar from a sieve over the petals and buds, coating them evenly.

▶ **Dry:** Leave to air dry at room temperature and, when crystallized and solid, carefully pack into an airtight container for freezer storage, or use immediately.

Did You Know?

Many flowers are poisonous. Just because you have seen food photography with flowers used for decoration, it does not mean that these are safe to eat.

Did You Know?

You can also flavour clear honey by adding rose petals (the same preparation applies). Leave the mix to steep for a week before use. Separate the petals from the honey by passing it through a sieve.

Rose-flavoured Sugar

There is a variety of natural flavourings that you can use for sugar, such as lavender and vanilla, and rose-petal sugar is similarly useful to have to hand in the kitchen. It can be used to dredge homemade cakes and biscuits, to flavour various creams, desserts and custards, or to add an interesting dimension to a fruit syrup drizzled over ice cream and fresh strawberries.

▶ **Select a jar:** Select a large, clean, dry jar with an airtight lid (such as a Kilner or Mason jar).

▶ **Pick your petals:** Pick and wash a couple of handfuls of highly fragrant rose petals. Rinse and lay out to dry on a clean tea towel or on pieces of absorbent kitchen paper.

▶ **Layer:** Sieve sufficient fine caster (superfine) sugar to fill the jar and place a layer in the base. Add a single layer of rose petals.

▶ **Leave:** Continue in this way until the jar is full. Seal and leave in a dark cupboard or pantry for about a week, or until the rose fragrance has started to flavour the sugar.

237

▶ **Sieve:** If you prefer, you can sieve the rose petals out of the sugar when it is ready to use.

Making an Ice Bowl

This is a great way to add interest at a dinner party or special celebration. It involves suspending rose petals and foliage in ice, creating a container to hold a dessert such as homemade rose petal ice cream. You can add other edible blooms if you prefer.

Here is how you make your own rose ice bowl:

▶ **Select your bowls:** Find a clear glass freezer-proof mixing bowl and another smaller glass or metal bowl to sit inside it, so that a gap of around 2 cm (¾ in) or slightly more is left between them when the rims of both bowls are held level.

▶ **Prepare the roses:** Collect and wash fresh, colourful and unblemished rose petals or small unfurling rose heads and a few leaves. In autumn, you could use rose hips and foliage.

▶ **Create the mould:** Part fill the larger bowl with water, remembering ice expands as it freezes, and position the smaller bowl in the centre, adding more water until the rim of the inner is at the same level as the outer. You can weigh the inner bowl down by adding water to it. Ensure the bowl rims are proud of the water.

▶ **Secure:** If the rims of the bowls are dry enough, use a few strips of sticky tape across the bowls to hold the inner bowl in the centre.

▶ **Add the decorations:** Slide the rose buds, petals and foliage down the sides using an implement to push the blooms lower.

▶ **Freeze:** Carefully transfer to the freezer and allow to solidify.

▶ **Release the mould:** Separate the ice bowl from the two halves of the mould by leaving it out at room temperature until the inner bowl can be twisted free. Upturn the ice bowl on a clean tea towel and carefully remove the larger half of the mould.

▶ **Prepare for use:** Keep in the freezer until ready for use and stand on a plate to catch the melt water. A folded piece of absorbent kitchen towel will stop the bowl rocking around on the plate.

Did You Know?

Large ice-cube trays, empty yogurt pots or mini jelly moulds can be used to make giant ice cubes featuring whole frozen roses or rose buds for table decorations at parties.

Rose-flavoured Ice Cream

You do not need an ice cream maker to create homemade ice cream. You just need an electric hand mixer, a food blender and some patience. Use your favourite basic ice-cream recipe, then flavour and colour as follows. This is an ideal dessert to serve in the rose ice bowl.

▶ **Rose flavouring:** Create the rose flavouring and colouring by making a tea of rose petals, using two cups of really dark pink or red petals (washed) in a small pan covered with 300 ml (1¼ cups) of water. Cover and simmer gently for 15 to 20 minutes, adding more water if necessary to keep the petals just covered.

▶ **Blend the mix:** There is no need to separate out the petals as you do for rose water. Just add to your ice-cream ingredients and mix in a blender. For more colour and texture, add some fresh pink or red petals and pulse the blender to chop them slightly.

▶ **Cold dish:** Chill a freezer-proof dish in the freezer and pour the mix into it, returning it to the freezer for around half an hour. After this time, test to see if it has started to freeze around the edges. If it has, it is time to take it out.

▶ **Beat:** Using the hand mixer, break up the frozen parts and create a smooth consistency. Put it back in the freezer and repeat the process four or five times, mixing to create a creamy blend. If it gets too hard at any time, let it thaw slightly in the fridge. Keep the ice cream in the freezer when the blending has been successfully completed.

Checklist

▶ **Cut flowers:** Roses last best if they are cut early or late in the day. Place in a deep bucket of water in a cool spot to condition for several hours.

▶ **Arrangements:** Strip off lower leaves and de-thorn. Lay out plant material, tools and sundries in front of you. Ensure containers are spotless.

▶ **Dried roses:** Pick roses in advanced bud stage and dry in a warm room. Dry fresh petals for weddings or crush slightly for potpourri.

▶ **Rose water and tea:** Gently heat rose petals in water, cool and sieve. Store as ice cubes. For tea, infuse fresh petals in boiled water and steep.

▶ **Fresh food decorations:** Use roses to decorate cakes, desserts and drinks. Make ice cubes containing whole rose buds.

▶ **Crystallized:** Use egg white and caster (superfine) sugar for candied rose buds and petals.

▶ **Rose sugar:** Infuse caster sugar for baking and dredging using layers of petals in a sealed jar.

▶ **Ice bowl:** Suspend flowers and leaves in ice to create a centrepiece for a dinner party.

▶ **Ice cream:** Make homemade ice cream flavoured with a 'tea' of rose petals.

Calendar of Care

Early Spring

Pruning and Deadheading

▶ Continue pruning bush roses, English roses and Modern Climbers.

▶ Shorten the stems of tall, repeat-flowering roses planted in windy gardens. If necessary, provide temporary stakes.

Planting and Mulching

▶ Finish planting bare-root roses and hedging.

▶ Mulch newly planted roses to conserve moisture during the growing season and reduce weeds.

▶ Replenish or add mulch to bush, shrub and climbing roses after pruning to help control pests and fungal diseases.

General Maintenance

▶ Check new plantings for wind rock and firm in.

▶ In cold regions, as temperatures increase and the ground thaws, remove insulation, piled up soil and mulches and bring buried bush roses back upright and firm in.

▶ Start returning patio planters of roses back to their original position and remove remaining insulation.

▶ Watch for signs of rabbits, deer and so on eating newly planted roses. Put up barriers if necessary.

▶ Feed roses in borders and in pots using a rose feed or a sustained-release granular fertilizer with added trace elements.

▶ Top dress roses in pots every couple of years, removing some of the compost and mulch and replacing with new.

Mid-spring

Pruning and Deadheading
▶ Cut out any damaged or dead wood.
▶ Remove suckers coming from below the graft union.

Planting and Mulching
▶ Plant container-grown roses in beds and borders (especially in cold regions).
▶ Finish mulching newly planted roses and hedges.
▶ Pot up new rose planters and mulch to conserve moisture.

General Maintenance
▶ Watch for signs of pests such as aphids or caterpillars on new growth and developing flower buds. Hand pick, rub off or blast off with a strong jet of water.
▶ Water if the spring season starts off dry, otherwise new growth may be retarded.
▶ Feed roses in cold regions if not already done.

Late Spring

Pruning and Deadheading

▶ Deadhead bush and shrub roses and large-flowered Old Garden roses.

Planting and Mulching

▶ Continue planting container-grown roses, provided the ground is moist and you can water in the weeks to come.

▶ Pot up new rose planters and mulch to conserve moisture.

General Maintenance

▶ Keep irrigation water off the stems and foliage of roses to reduce disease risk.

▶ Check ties on climbing roses and loosen any that are cutting into stems. Tie in new shoots as they grow.

▶ Put saucers under pots of roses to help keep compost moist. Remove if compost becomes too wet.

Early Summer

Pruning and Deadheading

▶ Prolong and improve displays of once-flowering shrub roses and Old Garden roses by deadheading regularly.

▶ Deadhead roses growing in containers.

Planting and Mulching

▶ Top up existing bark mulches that are wearing thin, but water thoroughly first or apply after rain.

▶ Continue planting container-grown roses, provided the ground is moist and you can water in the weeks to come.

244

General Maintenance

▶ Watch for early signs of black spot, rust and other fungi and pick off affected leaves or cut off shoots and pick up any fallen debris.

▶ Continue to be watchful for rose insect pests and take prompt action. Try organic insecticidal soap sprays for aphids.

▶ Water roses in drought conditions or in dry, free-draining soils, especially varieties prone to powdery mildew. Water new plantings every few days.

Mid-summer

Pruning and Deadheading

▶ Deadhead and lightly prune early-flowering shrub roses and once-flowering Old Garden roses, if necessary taking out some of the oldest shoots towards the base.

▶ Deadhead Floribunda and Hybrid Tea roses and, with taller plants that are not branching well, combine deadheading with a very light pruning to stimulate growth.

General Maintenance

▶ Continue fortnightly waterings for newly planted roses and any planted through the winter. Water roses during prolonged dry spells, especially on free-draining soils.

▶ Apply the second main feed: rose fertilizer or sustained-release feed with trace elements and minerals.

▶ Feed roses in pots and containers with granular fertilizer, liquid rose feeds or foliar feeds.

▶ Water container-grown roses regularly.

245

Late Summer

Pruning and Deadheading

▶ Prune Rambler roses.

▶ Finish pruning Old Garden roses and early
flowering hedges.

▶ Continue deadheading Modern bush and Patio
roses, climbers and repeat-flowering shrub roses.

Planting and Mulching

▶ Order new bare-root roses for planting in the
dormant season.

General Maintenance

▶ In cold regions, consider watering bush roses with
tomato food to help toughen up stems for the winter.

▶ Water in dry spells.

▶ Maintain pest and disease monitoring.

Early Autumn

Pruning and Deadheading

▶ Continue deadheading.

Planting and Mulching

▶ Plant container-grown roses to take advantage of damp autumn weather.

246

General Maintenance

▶ Tie in long shoots on climbers and Ramblers that have grown away from their supports.

▶ Water in dry spells.

▶ Control black spot and rust.

Mid-autumn

Pruning and Deadheading

▶ Continue deadheading late-flowering bush and climbing roses and take hardwood cuttings if you plan to propagate.

Planting and Mulching

▶ Start preparing ground for new plantings as well as hedges.

▶ In very cold areas, begin heaping mounds of soil and dry mulch material over roses to help insulate plants growing in borders.

▶ In areas where the winter is very dry, water roses before applying protective mulches.

General Maintenance

▶ Pick off leaves infected with black spot or rust and any diseased leaves that have fallen.

▶ Cut off any grey mould (botrytis) infected shoots and flower buds.

▶ Ensure the ground at the base of roses is clear of weeds and other plants to reduce risk of overwintering pests and diseases.

▶ Remove dishes from beneath patio pots.

247

Late Autumn

Pruning and Deadheading
▶ In windy areas, reduce the height of tall bush and shrub roses slightly to reduce wind rock, as well as very tall rose hedges.

Planting and Mulching
▶ Begin planting bare-root roses when available.

General Maintenance
▶ Tie in any branches on climbers and wall shrubs that have come adrift in the wind.

Early Winter

Pruning and Deadheading
▶ Remove remaining flowers to reduce risk of disease.

Planting and Mulching
▶ Continue planting bare-root roses and hedging.

General Maintenance
▶ Pick off any remaining leaves from black-spot-prone roses and collect leaf debris. This also helps roses go into winter dormancy.

Mid-winter

Pruning and Deadheading

▶ Carry out restoration pruning on overgrown shrub, Rambler and climbing roses.

▶ In mild, frost-free areas, prune bush and climbing roses.

▶ Clip over *Rosa rugosa* hedges, especially after the birds have eaten the hips.

Planting and Mulching

▶ Continue planting bare-root roses and hedging.

General Maintenance

▶ Check plants for wind rock. ▶ Ensure insulation against cold is still in place.

Late Winter

Pruning and Deadheading

▶ Begin pruning Modern bush and climbing roses, and English roses.

▶ Cut out dead or damaged wood on shrub roses and Ramblers. ▶ Trim repeat-flowering hedging.

Planting and Mulching

▶ Continue planting bare-root roses and hedging.

▶ Mulch new plantings and hedges. ▶ Top up existing mulches of manure or compost as well as bark.

▶ Lay down bark mulch to suppress weeds, applying general fertilizer beforehand.

General Maintenance

▶ Tidy up any debris and weeds to keep the ground beneath roses clear, ready for the season ahead.

Further Reading

Austin, D., *Climbing and Rambler Roses*, Garden Art Press, 2016

Austin, D., *The English Roses*, 2017

Austin, D., *The Rose*, Garden Art Press, 2013

Ed. by J. Cubey, J. Armitage, *RHS Plant Finder 2018*, Royal Horticultural Society, 2018

Eastoe, J., *Vintage Roses: Beautiful Varieties for Home and Garden*, Gibbs Smith, 2017

Elliott, B., *The Rose*, André Deutsch Ltd, 2016

R. 'Desdemona'

Green, D., *Tender Roses in Tough Climates: How to Grow Awesome Rose Garden Plants in the North (Beginner Gardening Book 6)*, (Kindle), 2012

Kukielski, P., *Roses Without Chemicals: 150 Disease-Free Varieties That Will Change the Way You Grow Roses*, Timber Press, 2015

Mikolajski, A., *Modern Roses: An Illustrated Guide to Varieties, Cultivation and Care, with Step-by-Step Instructions and Over 150 Beautiful Photographs*, Southwater, 2014

Palmstierna, I., *Practical Rose Gardening: How to Place, Plant, and Grow More Than Fifty Easy-Care Varieties*, Skyhorse Publishing, 2015

Quest-Ritson, B., Quest-Ritson, C., *American Rose Society Encyclopedia of Roses: The Definitive A-Z Guide*, Dorling Kindersley, 2003

Quest-Ritson, B., Quest-Ritson, C., *The Royal Horticultural Society Encyclopedia of Roses*, Dorling Kindersley, 2011

Royal Horticultural Society, *Roses (RHS Practicals)*, Dorling Kindersley, 2003

Schneider, P., *Right Rose, Right Place*, Storey Publishing, 2009

Zimmerman, P., *Everyday Roses*, Taunton, 2013

Websites

www.classicroses.co.uk
This is the webste for Peter Beales Roses, who have been growing since 1968 and are world-renowned for specializing in the preservation of old fashioned, historic and rare roses.

www.davesgarden.com
Claiming to be the 'hands down favourite website of gardeners around the world', this site offers gardening advice from members' forums and there is a comprehensive list of rose varieties in their 'PlantFiles' section.

www.davidaustinroses.co.uk
David Austin is one of the best-known contemporary breeders of roses. His website both sells his award-winning roses and offers advice on their care and cultivation.

www.edmundsroses.com
Supplier of roses within the US, offering both a huge collection of rose varieties and the tools and supplies needed to care for your roses after purchase.

www.finegardening.com
This is a gardening website with lots of articles on design and how-to. Perfect for weekend projects and DIY gardens.

www.gardeners.com/home
Garden supplies, gardening tools, and gardening tips, including articles with specific advice on roses.

www.gardeningknowhow.com
A great website for beginner gardeners but also with many articles dedicated to roses, including how to grow container roses. There is also a forum for posting questions.

www.planetnatural.com/rose-gardening-guru
An organic-growing site that gives advice and help on how to raise roses naturally, including organic pest and disease control.

www.realflowers.co.uk
The Real Flower Co. sells luxury bouquets of roses, flowers, herbs and foliage grown on their own sustainable farms.

www.rhs.org.uk
The Royal Horticultural Society's website, offering an extensive range of gardening advice, as well as a forum where you can post tips and have your queries answered.

www.rose.org
The American Rose Society's website, with accurate and current information on rose classification and varieties, as well as rose care. It advertises speaking events and meet-ups, so you can meet face-to-face with rose experts.

www.rosenotes.com
Run by a rose author, flower arranger, and garden designer, this site offers advice on where to source roses, how to care for them, and taking things further with your blooms.

www.rosesuk.com
Funded by the British Association of Rose Breeders, this website can be used to search for specific varieties of rose, as well as listing the rose suppliers available in the UK.

www.theherbalacademy.com/34-ways-to-use-roses
Great ideas on how to use your rose blooms once they have flowered, including both beauty and culinary uses.

Index